Par and Yardage

Hole	Par	Yardage	Hole	Par	Yardage
1	4	450	10	3	188
2	4	453	11	4	396
3	3	216	12	5	640
4	4	469	13	3	214
5	5	515	14	4	458
6	4	321	15	4	416
7	3	162	16	4	478
8	4	475	17	4	449
9	4	514	18	4	450
	35	3575		35	3689

106th
U.S. OPEN
Winged Foot

Written by Robert Sommers   **Photography by Getty Images**   **Edited by Bev Norwood**

ISBN 1-878843-45-1

Statistics produced by Unisys Corporation

Photographs ©Getty Images
Photograph on page 39, top left, ©USGA/John Mummert
Course illustrations by Dan Wardlaw ©The Majors of Golf

Published by IMG Worldwide Inc.,
1360 East Ninth Street, Cleveland, Ohio 44114

Designed and produced by Davis Design

Printed in the United States of America

In the days after the shocking finish to the U.S. Open at Winged Foot, I had a number of phone calls from golf writers and sportscasters, all involving Phil Mickelson's disaster at the 72nd hole, one, because many liken Phil's style of play to mine in my prime days and, two, because I lost a Masters in similar fashion in 1961.

I told them what I sincerely believe — that Mickelson is too good a player not to bounce back from what I know had to be a crushing emotional blow in the immediate aftermath of that sad ending. I did. I won four of my major titles and a total of 65 tournaments after I let that Masters title escape me in 1961. I expect Phil to do much the same.

But what I also told the callers was how impressed I was with how Geoff Ogilvy did what Phil and Colin Montgomerie and Jim Furyk could not do amid the tremendous pressure surrounding the final groups as they played that demanding 18th hole.

Although he has competed in America since 2001, this 29-year-old Australian was not a readily recognized player despite his PGA Tour win at Tucson in 2005 and more impressive victory in the Match Play Championship earlier in 2006. Yet, it hardly surprised Geoff's peers on Tour that he made that splendid 4 from in front of the green after Furyk had missed his four-foot par putt there and before Montgomerie made his double bogey from the middle of the fairway to come up a stroke short again in a major championship and Mickelson met his doom deep in the left rough and in the greenside bunker of that last hole. His fellow pros know how good he is.

Arnold Palmer

The seventh hole, par 3 and 162 yards.

The village of Mamaroneck lies along one of the major commuter rail lines into Manhattan, perhaps 45 minutes from the city's frenzied cadence. Large, impressive houses overlook narrow, winding streets lined with trees that arch across roadways, flowering shrubs that blossom in colors of red, pink, yellow or white, and weathered rail fences, more ornamental than functional. Lanes bearing picturesque names such as Carriage Way or Gate House Road hint of an earlier tranquil pace of life.

The main entrance to the Winged Foot Golf Club curls off Fenimore Road, a two-lane byway overtaxed only on those infrequent occasions when a major golf competition comes to town. Winged Foot has had its share of those — five U.S. Opens, two U.S. Amateurs and a PGA Championship on its West Course, the sturdier of the two, and two U.S. Women's Opens and the 1980 inaugural U.S. Senior Open on its East Course.

As its introduction to championship golf, barely six years after its founding, Winged Foot took on the 1929 United States Open Championship, an occasion so memorable it has enriched club lore for the better part of a century. This was the era of Bob Jones, the Atlanta amateur who ruled over championship golf in the 1920s. Other Opens followed — 1959, 1974, 1984 and 2006 — each with its own sense of drama. Yet for some members, the 1929 championship is still the most compelling.

By 1929, one year before his incomparable Grand Slam, Jones had won two U.S. Opens, two British Opens and four U.S. Amateur championships. As he strode onto the 15th tee in that final round, he led by three strokes. Up ahead, Al Espinosa, Jones's closest challenger, was about to finish with 75 and 294. No one still on the course had a chance. Three pars would bring Jones in at 291.

And yet nothing was certain. Jones had played loose golf earlier, pitching back and forth across the eighth green from one bunker to another and staggering off with a 7 on a par-4 hole. He recovered quickly, though, and played nearly flawless golf until the 15th, a modest par 4 of 397 yards with a quiet creek purling across the fairway about 270 yards out.

There he over-clubbed his approach, misjudged a soft lob that barely missed clearing a knoll, and before he knew it he had taken another 7. Now, instead of having strokes in hand, Jones needed to par the final three holes to score 294 and catch Espinosa. Then he bungled a birdie opportunity at the 16th, a 456-yard par 5, by three-putting after reaching the green with a long-iron second. Now, with two more pars to force a playoff, Jones could afford no more mistakes.

Safely past the 17th, he faced the home hole, a par 4 of 419 yards with its approach to a wide green set high above the fairway and protected by a dangerous bunker bordering its left flank. Jones played his drive nicely, but he pulled his approach toward the bunker. The ball barely missed the sand and nestled in rough grass. Now he must get down in two.

Taking an awkward stance, his feet above the ball, he played a niblick that pulled up 12 feet short and left him a difficult side-hill putt that would break about a foot and a half from left to right on a slippery green.

The first hole, par 4 and 450 yards.

A crowd estimated at 10,000 fans encircled the green and hushed as Jones studied his line. Finally satisfied, he set his putter behind the ball, then tapped it smartly. It ran straight for a time, took the break, hesitated as the gallery held its breath, then tumbled into the hole. Jones had forced a playoff. He and Espinosa would play 36 holes the next day.

It was no contest. Wildly off his game, Espinosa stumbled around in 80-84 while Jones, sharp as he had ever been, played the first round in 72, his second in 69, and with a score of 141 won the playoff by 23 strokes.

In the enthusiasm of the time, the writer Grantland Rice declared that nerveless stroke "Golf's Greatest Putt." He may have gone too far, but it remains about as important a putt as anyone has holed in the U.S. Open. Certainly it will never be forgotten around Winged Foot. The club took steps to assure it wouldn't.

Twenty-five years later Winged Foot invited Jones to return and celebrate that long-ago day with Tommy Armour, Gene Sarazen, Johnny Farrell and Craig Wood, all among that 1929 field and all of them Open champions. As part of the observance, those four played an exhibition match, and when it was over, they, along with a few others, gathered at the 18th green to recreate that dramatic moment in 1929. Partially handicapped by the disease that finally killed him, Jones pointed to the hole's position that afternoon, and the greenkeeper placed it there.

In turn, Armour, Sarazen, Farrell and Wood missed. They tried again, and again they missed. Then they called on Findlay Douglas, the 1898 U.S. Amateur champion and later the USGA president. He missed. So did Joe Dey, who had served many years as the USGA's Executive Director. No one holed it.

It is said that Jones declined to try, reminding everyone, "I've already made it."

All of this perpetuated the Jones legend.

This was the first of the Open championships for Winged Foot, each stirring in its own way. Billy

Casper, an underrated player, putted his way to the 1959 championship, then Hale Irwin won in 1974, one of the more difficult the Open had experienced, and 10 years later, in 1984, Fuzzy Zoeller beat Greg Norman in a playoff after Norman had holed out at the 72nd with a cross-country putt.

The 1959 championship began as if time had run backwards and Ben Hogan was still the cold, deadly, efficient scoring machine of earlier days. Two months shy of his 47th birthday, he began by blistering Winged Foot's first nine in 32 strokes.

1*st*
PAR 4
450 YARDS

2*nd*
PAR 4
453 YARDS

He could give no more, though. Just one stroke off the lead the morning of the last round, he faded to a 76 and tied for eighth (rain had interrupted the scheduled 36-hole final day on Saturday, and so for the first time the USGA scheduled the fourth round for Sunday).

This Open belonged to Billy Casper, a pudgy, 27-year-old Californian who weighed 212 pounds, enjoyed food and putted like a dream. While Hogan would hit green after green and come away with a two-putt par in that opening round, Casper one-putted eight greens and shot 71. Continuing in the second round, he missed the first green and holed from four feet for the par, drove into a bunker at the second and holed from eight feet, missed the third green with his tee shot and holed from nine feet, bunkered his approach to the fourth and saved another par from seven feet, then

ran in an 18-footer and birdied the fifth, a par 5. Since he had finished the first round with four consecutive one-putt greens, he had run his string to nine. Then, facing a 12-foot birdie chance at the sixth, somehow Casper missed.

Over four rounds, Casper one-putted 31 greens and two-putted 40. He scored 282 and won by one stroke over Bob Rosburg and by two over Mike Souchak and Claude Harmon, Winged Foot's professional.

Fifteen years later, when Winged Foot held the 1974 Open, the

3*rd*
PAR 3
216 YARDS

four-day championship had become standard. By then, too, a number of the better players grumbled that Tour courses had become so easy they need only swing hard, scrape the ball onto the green, and rely on a delicate putting stroke. Lee Trevino, a great maneuverer of the ball, lamented, "Finesse had been replaced by muscle," and the rough eliminated. "Sometimes," he said, "we get better lies in the rough than the fairway."

Irwin, the eventual winner, tried to dig his ball from the left rough of the 17th with a wooden club. He moved it maybe 100 yards. Still, he made his par with a pitch to 10 feet and a steady putt.

Just what they wanted? Maybe not.

After a taste of those conditions, players fumed that the USGA meant to humiliate them. Sandy Tatum, an eloquent lawyer from California who was then Chairman of the Championship Committee, rebutted that charge and answered: "We are not trying to humiliate the great players. We're trying to identify them," a statement now part of golf lore.

While younger men grumbled, 62-year-old Sam Snead played practice rounds of 71 on Monday and 72 on Tuesday. But just as impossible dreams spread through the gallery, Snead complained of chest pains and doctors rushed him to a hospital. They found he had cracked some ribs falling off a tractor on his Virginia farm. Of course he withdrew.

Nevertheless, the field turned in terrifying scores. Gene Littler and Billy Casper shot 80 in the opening round and Lee Trevino shot 78. After his own 78, John Schlee moaned, "I don't know whether to practice or cut my wrists."

Among the game's best long-iron players, Irwin won the championship with a score of 287, seven over par, the highest score in relation to par since Julius Boros, Jacky Cupit and Arnold Palmer

4th
PAR 4
469 YARDS

Then they arrived at Winged Foot and found punishing rough, hard and quick greens, narrow fairways, holes demanding lots of long-iron shots and adventurous putting. Faced with a downhill 20-footer at the first hole, Jack Nicklaus tapped his ball gently and watched horrified as it glided past the hole and scooted off the green. On another hole, Johnny Miller lined up with his back to the hole — to see how it looked over his left shoulder. So firm were they that vandals drove a car over the first green the evening after the opening round without leaving a trace. No one noticed except the men who set the holes early the next morning.

The rough, always devilish in the Open, stood five inches high just six feet off narrow fairways. Playing more than a 4-iron from this stuff tempted ruin. Leading the field with two holes to play, Hale

5th
PAR 5
515 YARDS

The sixth hole, par 4 and 321 yards.

tied at 293, a score of nine over par, in 1963 at The Country Club, in Brookline, Mass. That Open, though, had been played on a course damaged by a wicked winter, vandals who slashed messages on greens and fluky, windy weather.

The 1974 championship evolved into a battle between Irwin and Forest (Fuzzy) Fezler, a relatively obscure player who went into the final round at 219, five strokes behind Irwin and six behind a young Tom Watson, who hadn't yet learned how to close. Watson fizzled with a final round of 79.

Fezler played the first 17 holes in one under par, but he pulled his drive into the left rough and bogeyed the 18th. With 70, one of the lowest scores of the week, Fezler finished at 289. Irwin, meanwhile, had gone out in 36, one above par, but he parred just one of the next seven holes, birdied two and bogeyed four, a loss of two more strokes.

By the time Irwin reached the 18th tee, Fezler had finished, and Irwin closed out in style — a solid drive, a heroic 2-iron dead on line, and two putts for the par. With 73, he had clipped Fezler by two strokes. This was Irwin's first Open championship. He would win a second in 1979 and another in 1990.

6th
PAR 4
321 YARDS

7th
PAR 3
162 YARDS

Later in the year, the author Dick Schaap published a book titled *Massacre at Winged Foot* portraying the course setup as so beyond reason it demeaned the good players. A simple glance at the results destroyed Schaap's claim. Of the low 11 scorers (11 because Brian Allin tied Jack Nicklaus for 10th place), seven had already won the Open or soon would. They were, in the order of their finish, Irwin, of course, who would win two more, Lou Graham, who would win the following year, Arnold Palmer (1960), Tom Watson (1982), Tom Kite (1992), Gary Player (1965), and Jack Nicklaus, who had won three by then and would win again six years later. Most of them won other of the game's premier events, which certainly validates the course setup, severe though it might have been.

Ten years passed before Winged Foot held another Open, and we almost saw a repeat of 1929. Before the championship began, the USGA and the club agreed to place the hole at 18 in the same location for the fourth round as it had been in Jones's day. By chance, playing the fourth round with the championship at stake, Greg Norman reprised that dramatic putt and tied Fuzzy Zoeller. Unlike Jones, though, Norman lost the playoff.

With the course much more playable than in 1974, the scores ran lower. Norman opened with 70 and followed with 68-69-69 while Zoeller played Winged Foot in 71-66-69-70. Where Irwin had won the 1974 championship with 287, Zoeller and Norman tied at 276, 11 strokes lower.

Playing immediately ahead of Zoeller, Norman stepped onto the 18th tee one under par, even with Zoeller. Norman, though, had been prone to lose critical shots to the right, and here he pushed his approach into a grandstand. Allowed to drop a ball without penalty from a temporary immovable obstruction, he pitched to the far side of the green. From about the same dis-

8th
PAR 4
475 YARDS

9th
PAR 4
514 YARDS

The 10th hole, par 3 and 188 yards.

tance and angle as Jones so many years earlier, he rolled it in for the 4 and 69.

Just now catching up and not realizing Norman had simply parred the 18th and not birdied, Fuzzy waved a towel in surrender. Quickly, though, the gallery let him know Norman had putted for a 4, not a 3. Fuzzy then made his 4, tied Norman, and the next day won the playoff easily with 67 against Norman's 75.

Over the years, Winged Foot has held its place among the more challenging tests of golf, all the while remaining largely unchanged. For a time greens had been shrunk to reduce maintenance costs during the Great Depression of the

1930s, although many have recently been restored close to their original size, and more lately occasionally lengthened under the constant pressure of evolving equipment. Winged Foot West measured 6,786 yards in the days of hickory shafts and wobbly balls. For the Open's 2006 renewal it had been stretched out to 7,264 yards, the longest Open course ever.

An Open course of 7,000 yards, though, doesn't break precedent. As far back as 1965, Bellerive Country Club, in St. Louis, stretched to 7,191 yards. Still, 25

10*th*
PAR 3
188 YARDS

11

years passed before the next 7,000-yard course. Medinah Country Club, in Chicago, measured 7,195 yards in 1990. Gary Player won at Bellerive and Hale Irwin at Medinah, neither exceptionally long hitters.

Prepping the course for the 2006 Open, Winged Foot added 105 yards to its 12th, turning a 535-yard hole into a monstrous par 5 of 640 yards. Still, statistics show it as one of the easier pars. Additionally, the third, which had remained a 216-yard par 3 throughout the time, lengthened to 243 yards in the third round in 2006, and it surren-

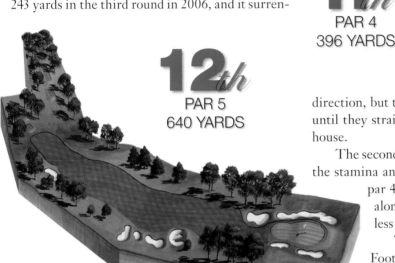

11th
PAR 4
396 YARDS

12th
PAR 5
640 YARDS

dered just 16 birdies, although Sweden's Peter Hedblom scored a hole-in-one during the third round. Most of the holes played largely the same, although the club added almost 50 yards to the ninth, changing it from 446 yards to 514 yards, yet holding its par to 4. Over the four days it surrendered 26 birdies and one eagle.

The West Course doesn't exactly creep up on you. Beginning from the club's elegant clubhouse, itself a work of art built of gray stone scraped up clearing ground for the golf course, it opens with a 450-yard par 4 that turns slightly left. A slightly longer par 4 follows, then the 216-yard par 3. The first three run practically in the same

direction, but then the holes weave back and forth until they straighten for the run back to the clubhouse.

The second nine is no easier, and its finish tests the stamina and resolve of the best players — five par 4s that range from 416 to 478 yards, along with a 214-yard par 3 and the endless 640-yard 12th.

Through years of testing, Winged Foot has proved itself among the finest of the game's parkland courses, with its variety of holes, its immaculate conditioning and its rich selection of trees, suitable for an arboretum. It has long par 4s and short par 4s, a par 5

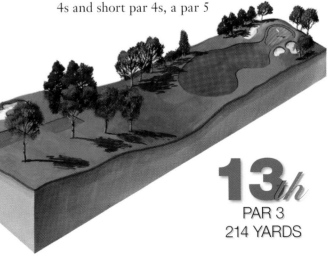

13th
PAR 3
214 YARDS

The 11th hole, par 4 and 396 yards.

that the ordinary Tour player can reach routinely with his second shots and a par 5 that challenges him, and par 3s that call for medium irons for some and others that demand more.

Organized in 1921 by a group of New York Athletic Club members, they chose the golf club's name from NYAC's emblem: a winged foot. Searching for suitable land, the club's founders settled on a tract of soft green meadowland salted with outcroppings of rock scraped down by the great glacier of the Ice Age and covered with this vast variety of trees. The holes of both courses wander through stands of oak and maple, linden and ash, birch and beech, pines, spruce, golden raintree, and the flowering trees white and pink dogwood, purplish Japanese lilac and the vividly red eastern redbud.

When they explored the site they realized they had ample land for two courses and arranged for construction to begin in May of 1921. Two years later, in June of 1923, all 36 holes opened.

To design and build their courses, they chose A.W. Tillinghast, a genius at his craft. When they

walked into his office on New York's 42nd Street, they told him, "Give us a man-sized course." He followed his mission and gave them two.

Mercurial and outrageous, Albert Warren Tillinghast ranks among the great designers of golf courses. Born in 1874 to a privileged family, he grew up near Philadelphia, the son of a manufacturer of rubber goods who adored him. Consequently, Tillie grew up spoiled and undisciplined, upbringing that may not have been best for the family but possibly sparked his creative instincts. The free-thinking brat grew into a man of remarkable and entertaining talents.

He played a decent game of golf, wrote a syndicated column about the game, ranked the nation's leading amateur, professional and women players (in 1916 he placed 14-year-old Bobby Jones 12th and predicted a great future for the boy), contributed to and later edited the magazine *Golf Illustrated*, photographed golf subjects, collected golf art and other memorabilia, and promoted and organized golf events. He put together the Shawnee Open

14th
PAR 4
458 YARDS

and Five Farms, in Baltimore, along with Baltusrol's Lower and Winged Foot West have held PGA Championships.

Among his other credits, Ridgewood, in Ridgewood, N.J.; Quaker Ridge, in Scarsdale, N.Y., one of the game's best unknown courses; Sunnehanna, in Johnstown, and Shawnee, in Shawnee, Pa.; Oklahoma City Golf and Country Club; San Francisco Golf Club; and Brackenridge Park, in San Antonio.

While he prospered through the Roaring Twenties, the Great Depression ended the good times and more courses closed than opened. Those who built

that 21-year-old Johnny McDermott won in 1913.

He drank heavily, occasionally disappeared for a month or more, and at times behaved disgustingly. When he was in the mood he could charm the quills off a porcupine. He played the piano, showed a talent for sketching, talked like a dream and knew a wide assortment of prominent people.

Eccentric perhaps, but Tillinghast had a remarkably diverse influence over golf. He created wonderful courses that featured wide and generous fairways and tightly bunkered greens that demanded precise iron play, and he was among the first to link construction with design. If you hired Tillinghast to design your course, you hired Tillinghast Construction to build it.

15th
PAR 4
416 YARDS

them had little future, and because of his lifestyle, Tillie found himself especially vulnerable. When he'd had money, he had spent it. Now he had nothing. He eventually left golf and ended his days as an antique dealer in Beverly Hills.

Tillinghast's design business thrived through the 1920s, when he did most of his work, and during that time he gave us many of our classic golf courses. Consider his legacy:

Along with the four courses at Winged Foot and Baltusrol, he laid out 67 others in 17 states and three more in Canada. They include Fresh Meadow Country Club, on Long Island, both the Upper and Lower courses at Baltusrol and Winged Foot West. Each held U.S. Opens. Hermitage, in Richmond, Va., Pittsburgh Field Club,

16th
PAR 4
478 YARDS

The 14th hole, par 4 and 458 yards.

The 18th hole, par 4 and 450 yards.

A Dandy he may have been, but Tillinghast took his work seriously, concentrating on the approach to his putting greens. Summing up, he said:

"I feel I have never attempted a more important contribution to golf course construction," he wrote, "than this: the immaculate preparations of approaches to greens. In recent years I have devoted almost the same attention to contouring these as I have to the putting greens themselves."

Through Tillinghast's philosophy, Winged Foot has endured for 83 years, but as all the game's classic playgrounds it felt the challenge of modern equipment that altered the original design. Consequently we've had the steady creep of additional length, and for the Open, taller and more menacing rough. In order to prevent galleries from tramping down grass bordering fairways, Winged Foot removed about 600 trees as well, allowing a wider swath of rough.

Setting up the course, the USGA narrowed fairways and shaved the greens to high speeds, aiming for Stimpmeter speeds of 12 feet for most holes, but 10½ for the first because of its severe slopes. They didn't seem that fast, perhaps because the poa annua grass flowers at that time of year and grows quickly.

Some fairways had been squeezed to 22 yards with others as wide as 29 yards. At the extreme, the fairway of the 18th, which played to 450 yards, shrank to 23 yards, then to 22 at the sprinkler head 160 yards short of the green.

Rough abutting these fairways reached new heights — literally — and new toughness. Back in 1997 when Davis Love III won the PGA Championship at Winged Foot, thin-bladed fescue grass covered the rough. Two years before the 2006 Open, the club spread 32,000 pounds of coarse-bladed rye and bluegrass over the grounds. Now escape from the tall grass called for the conservative approach. Phil Mickelson will agree.

The usual 1½-inch first cut continued on every hole, then four inches of primary rough alongside all but the fifth, sixth and par-5 11th and a pair of par 4s of 321 and 396 yards. There the rough grew to six inches. The rough around the sixth green varied from six to eight inches, the most severe in living memory.

Winged Foot did indeed present a severe challenge to the Open field, but isn't playing their best under severe conditions how the great players identify themselves?

17th
PAR 4
449 YARDS

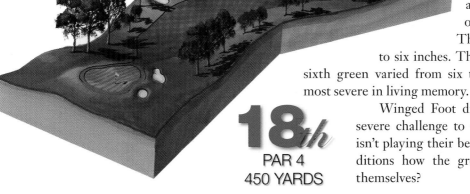

18th
PAR 4
450 YARDS

Interest in the qualifying was focused on a 16-year-old girl, Michelle Wie, who had five strokes too many.

106th
U.S. OPEN
Qualifying

The parking lot at the Short Hills Mall began filling up rather earlier than on a normal shopping day on June 5. Many of the folks who climbed from their cars that day came not to pillage those swank emporia but rather to watch a 16-year-old girl perhaps add a new chapter to the lore of the ancient game of golf.

They had come to watch Michelle Wie, already a professional and contending for the LPGA's top prizes, attempt to win a place in the 2006 United States Open Championship. She had passed through local qualifying and now had to compete against 143 others at the Canoe Brook Country Club for a prize no woman had ever sought.

More than 8,500 golfers had entered the Open. Some entrants faced both local and sectional rounds, but 265 entrants would skip the local and compete only in sectional qualifiers. Of the 815 players in the sectional rounds, just 76 would survive and join the 80 fully exempt in the starting field of 156 for the Open proper at Winged Foot.

The 36-hole qualifying test at Canoe Brook would be played over the club's North and South courses in Summit, N.J. It turned into quite a day.

Estimated at 3,000, a gallery packed with young and old people swarmed over the two courses. The press joined in the frenzy. Perhaps 300 representing the writing press and radio and television showed up. The Golf Channel broke into other programs with progress reports and produced an evening broadcast that ran from 7 until 10 p.m. covering all 13 qualifying competitions. *The New York Times* devoted more than a full page of text and pictures to the qualifying round, not quite as much as the daily coverage for the Open itself, but close.

For a time Wie had a chance. In her morning round Michelle shot two-under 68 over the South Course, the easier of the two. Deep into the second round she lay only a stroke away from winning a place. Then she ruined her day by dropping strokes on three consecutive holes. She played the second round in 75, turned in a score of 143, where she needed 138 to make the playoff. A score of 69 would have qualified, a 70 would have earned a place in a playoff.

While Wie struggled against players with much more experience at high levels, back in Hawaii, her home state, 15-year-old, 5-foot-1 Tadd Fujikawa, an amateur, shot 71-70–141, beat nine others and won the single place available. A few days later, the USGA discovered that Fujikawa was the youngest qualifier ever. He was several months younger than another 15-year-old, Tyrell Garth, had been when he qualified in 1941. The confirmation came in a telephone call to Garth's son in Beaumont, Texas.

In Columbus, Ohio, one of the two places at Double Eagle Golf Club went to Madalitso Muthiya, a 23-year old citizen of Zambia, the former Northern Rhodesia. He became the first from his country ever to qualify. Muthiya attended the University of New Mexico for four years on a golf scholarship and then moved on to the Canadian Tour. He won his place in the Open with rounds of 65 and 69, his 134 total four strokes better than Stephen Woodard, the other qualifier. Neither survived the 36-hole cut at Winged Foot.

Steve Stricker, who did make the cut and actually threatened to win, won his place by shooting 65 and 64 at the St. Charles (Ill.) Country Club. His 129 led all the scoring in the qualifying rounds.

Players Who Were Fully Exempt for the 2006 U.S. Open (80)

Robert Allenby	16	Bob Estes	8	Paul McGinley	10, 16
Steven Ames	6, 11, 16	Niclas Fasth	10, 16	Billy Mayfair	9
Stuart Appleby	9, 11, 16	Kenneth Ferrie	10	Rocco Mediate	8
Rich Beem	5	Fred Funk	9, 16	Shaun Micheel	5
Thomas Bjorn	10, 16	Jim Furyk	1, 9, 11, 12, 16	Phil Mickelson	3, 5, 9, 11, 12, 16
Olin Browne	9	Sergio Garcia	8, 9, 10, 16	Edoardo Molinari	2
Bart Bryant	9, 16	Lucas Glover	9, 16	Colin Montgomerie	10, 16
Angel Cabrera	10, 16	Retief Goosen	1, 8, 9, 10, 11, 16	Arron Oberholser	8, 16
Mark Calcavecchia	9	Todd Hamilton	4	Sean O'Hair	9
Chad Campbell	9, 11, 16	Padraig Harrington	9, 16	Nick O'Hern	15, 16
Michael Campbell	1, 8, 10, 16	Peter Hedblom	8	Jose Maria Olazabal	10, 16
Paul Casey	13, 16	Mark Hensby	8	Geoff Ogilvy	11, 16
K.J. Choi	8, 16	Tim Herron	9, 16	Rod Pampling	16
Stewart Cink	8, 16	Charles Howell III	9	Corey Pavin	8
Darren Clarke	16	David Howell	10, 13, 16	Kenny Perry	9, 16
Tim Clark	8, 9, 16	Ryuji Imada	8	Carl Pettersson	12
John Cook	8	Trevor Immelman	16	Nick Price	8
Fred Couples	8, 16	Peter Jacobsen	8	Ted Purdy	9
Ben Crane	9, 16	Lee Janzen	1	Rory Sabbatini	11, 16
Ben Curtis	4	Miguel Angel Jimenez	10, 16	Adam Scott	9, 15, 16
Chris DiMarco	9, 16	Brandt Jobe	9	Vijay Singh	5, 8, 9, 16
Luke Donald	9, 10, 16	Zach Johnson	16	Henrik Stenson	10, 16
Dillon Dougherty	2	Steve Jones	1	David Toms	5, 8, 9, 11, 16
Nick Dougherty	10	Shingo Katayama	14, 16	Scott Verplank	9, 16
Allen Doyle	7	Tom Lehman	16	Mike Weir	3, 16
David Duval	4	Justin Leonard	9	Tiger Woods	1, 3, 4, 8, 9,
Ernie Els	1, 4, 8, 16	Davis Love III	8, 9, 16		11, 12, 16

Key to Player Exemptions:

1. Winners of the U.S. Open Championship for the last 10 years.
2. Winner and runner-up of the 2005 U.S. Amateur Championship.
3. Winners of the Masters Tournament the last five years.
4. Winners of the British Open Championship the last five years.
5. Winners of the PGA of America Championship the last five years.
6. Winner of the 2006 Players Championship.
7. Winner of the 2005 U.S. Senior Open Championship.
8. From the 2005 U.S. Open Championship, the 15 lowest scorers and anyone tying for 15th place.
9. From the 2005 final official PGA Tour money list, the top 30 money leaders.
10. From the 2005 final official PGA European Tour, the top 15 money leaders.
11. From the 2006 official PGA Tour money list, the top 10 money leaders through May 29.
12. Any multiple winner of PGA Tour co-sponsored events whose victories are considered official from April 27, 2005 through June 4, 2006.
13. From the 2006 PGA European Tour, the top two money leaders through May 30.
14. From the 2005 final Japan Golf Tour money list, the top two leaders provided they are within the top 75 point leaders of the World Rankings at that time.
15. From the 2005 final PGA Tour of Australasia money list, the top two leaders provided they are within the top 75 point leaders of the World Rankings at that time.
16. From the World Rankings list, the top 50 point leaders as of May 30, 2006.
17. Special exemptions selected by the USGA Executive Committee. International players not otherwise exempt as selected by the USGA Executive Committee.

Sectional Qualifying Results

Tokyo Golf Club
Sayama City, Japan
67 players for 3 spots
Toru Taniguchi	70 - 66 – 136
Keiichiro Fukabori	69 - 69 – 138
(P)Tadahiro Takayama	67 - 72 – 139

Lake Merced Golf Club
Daly City, Calif.
67 players for 4 spots
Michael Derminio	70 - 68 – 138
*Taylor Wood	64 - 75 – 139
(P)*Alex Coe (a)	69 - 71 – 140
(P)*Patrick Nagle	73 - 67 – 140

St. Charles Country Club
St. Charles, Ill.
33 players for 2 spots
Steve Stricker	65 - 64 – 129
Jason Allred	71 - 63 – 134

Columbine Country Club
Littleton, Colo.
25 players for 1 spot
Dustin White	67 - 68 – 135

Tadd Fujikawa

Walton Heath Golf Club
Surrey, England
71 players for 8 spots
Maarten Lafeber	64 - 66 – 130
Graeme Storm	69 - 69 – 138
Graeme McDowell	70 - 68 – 138
Jyoti Randhawa	71 - 67 – 138
Richard Green	72 - 67 – 139
Jeev Milkha Singh	70 - 69 – 139
(P)Oliver Wilson	71 - 69 – 140
(P)Phillip Archer	69 - 71 – 140

Poipu Bay Golf Club
Koloa, Hawaii
10 players for 1 spot
*Tadd Fujikawa	71 - 70 – 141

Woodmont Country Club
Rockville, Md.
51 players for 4 spots
Tommy Armour III	68 - 67 – 135
Joey Sindelar	70 - 66 – 136
David Berganio Jr.	70 - 67 – 137
(P)Chad Collins	69 - 68 – 137

Toru Taniguchi

Canoe Brook Country Club
Summit, N.J.

153 players for 18 spots

Brett Quigley	68 - 63 – 131
Gregory Kraft	67 - 67 – 134
Kent Jones	66 - 68 – 134
Kevin Stadler	66 - 68 – 134
Michael Harris	68 - 66 – 134
J.J. Henry	70 - 65 – 135
Mark Brooks	68 - 67 – 135
Rob Johnson	66 - 69 – 135
Andy Bare	70 - 66 – 136
John Mallinger	68 - 68 – 136
Nicholas Thompson	69 - 67 – 136
Tom Pernice Jr.	68 - 68 – 136
Andrew Svoboda	72 - 65 – 137
Chris Nallen	69 - 68 – 137
David Oh	67 - 70 – 137
Phil Tataurangi	71 - 66 – 137
Scott Hend	68 - 69 – 137
(P)Brad Fritsch	72 - 66 – 138

Camilo Villegas

Brookside Golf and Country Club and Lakes Golf and Country Club
Columbus, Ohio

144 players for 21 spots

Benjamin Hayes	67 - 64 – 131
Ian Poulter	65 - 66 – 131
Bo Van Pelt	66 - 69 – 135
Charley Hoffman	65 - 70 – 135
Stephen Gangluff	65 - 70 – 135
Woody Austin	66 - 69 – 135
Camilo Villegas	67 - 69 – 136
Charl Schwartzel	70 - 66 – 136
J.B. Holmes	70 - 66 – 136
Jeff Sluman	65 - 71 – 136
Mathew Goggin	66 - 71 – 137
Skip Kendall	70 - 67 – 137
Steve Lowery	64 - 73 – 137
Craig Barlow	71 - 67 – 138
Dean Wilson	69 - 69 – 138
Nathan Green	69 - 69 – 138
D.J. Trahan	71 - 68 – 139
Jay Haas	69 - 70 – 139
John Rollins	72 - 67 – 139
Tag Ridings	70 - 69 – 139
(P)Duffy Waldorf	68 - 72 – 140

Ian Poulter

Jay Haas

Brett Quigley

Double Eagle Golf Club
Columbus, Ohio

37 players for 2 spots

Madalitso Muthiya	65 - 69 – 134
Stephen Woodard	70 - 68 – 138

Emerald Valley Golf Club
Creswell, Ore.
25 players for 1 spot
(P)*Jonathan Moore   70 - 67 –137

Lakeside Golf Club
Houston, Texas
32 players for 2 spots
*Ryan Baca   67 - 69 –136
*Ryan Posey   65 - 71 –136

Bo Van Pelt

Madalitso Muthiya

Matt Kuchar

Skip Kendall

Old Memorial Golf Club
Tampa, Fla.
59 players for 3 spots
John Koskinen   71 - 69 –140
*Billy Horschel   73 - 67 –140
(P)George McNeill   70 - 71 –141

Ansley Golf Club
(Settindown Creek Course)
Atlanta, Ga.
65 players for 4 spots
Jason Dufner   67 - 68 –135
Matt Kuchar   68 - 67 –135
Lee Williams   68 - 68 –136
Andrew Morse   67 - 70 –137

Fox Run Golf Club
St. Louis, Mo.
27 players for 2 spots
Travis Hurst   70 - 67 –137
(P)Jay Delsing   71 - 71 –142

*Denotes amateur   (P) Won playoff

After a rocky start, with bogeys on the first and third holes, Colin Montgomerie shot 69, the only below-par score.

The word subtle doesn't fit a description of Winged Foot's first hole. It's all there for you to see: 450 yards from the tee to a treacherous green with a narrow opening canted from back to front that promises nightmarish putting.

It doesn't ask for the artillery salvo of a John Daly sailing into dangerous territory, but rather the precision of Robin Hood's bow. Hitting the target — the fairway — must supersede any thought of distance. Cases in point:

In mid-morning of the U.S. Open's first round, Retief Goosen pushed his drive off the first tee into gnarly rough maybe six or seven yards from the pristine fairway. Now Goosen is no weakling, but grass this tall, perhaps five to six inches high, should frighten the bravest heart. As he approached his ball, Goosen gazed down at his lie, looked at the green in the distance, felt the fresh wind bearing toward him, and chose caution over bravado. He played a safe shot into the fairway and banked on a pitch and a putt to save a par 4. He succeeded.

Some time later Tiger Woods pushed his first drive into the same general area, but he chose disdain over caution, ripped into his ball with a vicious swing, missed the green, as had Goosen, but failed to save his par. Spectators standing nearby claimed he was lucky he didn't break bones in his hand. Then he bogeyed the second and the third holes and put himself in jeopardy from the start.

At the end of a bright, windy and surprising day, only Colin Montgomerie played under the par of 70. With his upright swing that has never changed, he eased around that exacting course in 69 strokes, one stroke better than the five men who

tied for second place and two ahead of eight others at 71. Phil Mickelson shot 70, along with Jim Furyk, Steve Stricker, Miguel Angel Jimenez and David Howell. Two strokes behind Montgomerie, Australia's Geoff Ogilvy came in with 71 and tied with the Englishman Kenneth Ferrie. Largely unknown in the United States, Ferrie would remain a contender to the end.

Vijay Singh shot 71 as well. A week earlier he had won the PGA Tour event at Westchester Country Club, just six miles from Winged Foot.

Showing little of the precision he demonstrated at Pinehurst when he won the Open a year earlier, Michael Campbell began the 2006 championship with a mundane 75. Still, the Open had barely begun, and even with his score he had a one-stroke lead over Woods, the winner in 2000 and 2002, and two strokes over Goosen, the 2001 and 2004 champion, who stumbled around the course in 77, leaving him in a tie for 90th place.

Generally, Winged Foot played tough; most of the field scored 75 or higher. Davis Love III had won the 1997 PGA Championship over this course with a 72-hole score of 269, but on his return visit he shot 76, leaving him tied for 68th place along with Woods and a slew of others. Carl Pettersson had won the Memorial Tournament with three rounds in the 60s but shot 77 at Winged Foot; Tom Pernice, tied for fifth a week earlier, had 79; and after a 79 of his own, David Toms withdrew.

In the minds of the gallery, though, all this meant little compared to the disappointing golf of Woods. He had scored as high as 76 only four times as a professional in one of the game's premier events. He shot 76s in the 2003 Masters and 2004

Local player and Winged Foot member Andrew Svoboda had the honor of the first tee shot on No. 1 at exactly 7 a.m.

Open, and he shot 77 in the 1998 British Open. On a miserable cold, rainy, windswept day four years earlier, Woods shot 81 at Muirfield in the third round of the British Open. He had bettered that score at Winged Foot, and with a decent second round he might have contended for his third U.S. Open title.

Woods could have missed the adrenaline high of competition. He hadn't played a round of competitive golf since the Masters in early April when he tied for third place with 284, three strokes behind Mickelson. Shortly after, Earl Woods, Tiger's father, had died of cancer. It had not been sudden; his death had been expected for months. Still, it hurt Woods badly. He and his father had been quite close, and it had been Earl who steered his son to golf and guided him throughout his career, watching him become the finest golfer of his time.

Woods had played in 11 U.S. Opens before coming to Winged Foot and only twice turned in a score so high. In 1996, still an amateur, he played the third round at Oakland Hills, in Detroit, in 77

and, more recently, he shot 76 in the last round at Shinnecock Hills in 2004. Never, though, twice in one championship.

He began with his drive into the deepest rough and his failed attempt to reach the green. From there he pitched onto a green tilted from back to front, and faced with a 10-foot putt to save his par, he missed. His game didn't improve. He missed the second green as well and left a downhill six-foot putt two feet short, but he reached the third, a 216-yard par 3 with a green protected by bunkers on both sides. Now 30 feet from the hole, he missed his first putt by six feet, then missed the next. Three consecutive bogeys.

This was not the Woods we all knew. He had lost control of his driver, his short game was rusty, and his putting uncertain. Still, he had some fight in him. He missed the fairway and the green of the fourth but scratched out a par 4, then revived hope by birdieing the fifth, the first of the par 5s. He reached the green with his second shot and two-putted. He was just two over par now, and maybe

First Round

Colin Montgomerie	69	-1
Jim Furyk	70	E
Phil Mickelson	70	E
Steve Stricker	70	E
Miguel Angel Jimenez	70	E
David Howell	70	E
Kenneth Ferrie	71	+1
Graeme McDowell	71	+1
Vijay Singh	71	+1
Mike Weir	71	+1
John Cook	71	+1
Fred Funk	71	+1
Kevin Stadler	71	+1
Geoff Ogilvy	71	+1

Miguel Angel Jimenez (70) credited his patience.

back on his game. Quickly, though, he gave away that stroke at the sixth, a straightaway par 4 of just 321 yards, a hole he could drive. Once again he missed the fairway and once again his pitch scooted over the green into heavy rough. He took two putts for his fourth bogey in six holes. His golf had become painful to watch.

Another stroke was lost at the eighth where Woods missed from 12 feet, and from the rough on the ninth, once again he swung viciously and flew his second shot into a grandstand. Showing charity to one who needed it, a young girl tossed the ball to him, he took a drop without penalty, overshot the green, chipped within six feet and for a change holed the putt for 5. Another stroke was lost. Woods had played the first nine in 40 strokes, five over par.

The homeward nine treated Woods more kindly — except for the 12th, the 640-yard par 5. Once more he drove into the rough, chopped his ball out, hit his third into a greenside bunker, his recovery ran over the green into heavy rough, and he missed an eight-foot putt for a bogey 6. He walked off with a 7. Seven over par now, Woods played the last six holes in one under par, came back in 36, and with 76 he trailed 67 others. Clearly he would have to improve to survive the 36-hole cut.

Over the course of the round, Woods had hit

Tiger Woods (76) was in trouble from the first hole.

Graeme McDowell (71) was excited by his play.

Michael Campbell (75) played well 'tee to green.'

Fred Funk (71) missed only three fairways.

David Howell (70) and his caddie discuss strategy.

just three fairways on the 14 driving holes and 10 greens. His putting, which had saved him occasionally, had been far below his normal standard. He three-putted just once, at the third hole, but he had one-putted just four. Altogether he had 33 putts, a rare figure for him.

Upset with his performance and angry at the course, Woods blamed the greens for his poor round. "You're used to playing U.S. Opens with fast greens," he said. "These aren't…Our group had a hard time with the speed…You don't normally see that with guys who are decent putters."

A number of other players complained about the greens, but Montgomerie handled them rather well. Where Woods needed 33 putts, Monty needed just 25, and while Woods hit only three fairways, Montgomerie reached nine in regulation figures, not an overwhelming number but good enough this day.

Off from the first tee at 8:28 in the morning, he had finished his round before Woods had begun, but Monty had almost as rocky a start. He

Mike Weir (71) was in the fairway on 10 tee shots.

lost strokes at both the first, Winged Foot's most difficult par, and the third, the par 3, missing the greens of both and the fairway of the first. He played an erratic first nine, making his pars on just three holes, but he turned for home just one over par, then putted like a dream. He needed just one putt on five holes, one of them rather spectacular.

Facing a 25-foot putt at the 17th, a 449-yard par 4, Montgomerie broke into a wide grin when it fell for a birdie 3. With a shorter birdie opening at the 18th, he missed from five feet.

Later, talking about those two putts, Monty dismissed any notion the missed putt on No. 18 had upset him.

"Oh," he said, "that putt broke a mile. I can't be worried about that. I was still enjoying the putt on 17. I hit that putt, and about halfway to the hole I thought, 'Well, that has no chance.' But it kept curling and it went in."

Just a week away from his 43rd birthday, Montgomerie had mellowed. Often touchy and irritable in the past, he joked more easily, smiled often and

Jim Furyk (70) hit only 10 greens but had 27 putts.

Phil Mickelson (70) made a birdie at the seventh.

Geoff Ogilvy (71) had consecutive birdies at 10 and 11.

seemed to enjoy bantering with the press. Asked about how the gallery treated him, he said, "I had a lot of support.

"I didn't need my *Golf Digest* badge, thank goodness." Then, grinning, he quipped innocently, "I don't know why they made so many."

For the 2002 Open, at Bethpage State Park, on Long Island, the magazine distributed 25,000 badges urging, "Be Nice to Monty."

The gallery had indeed encouraged Montgomerie throughout the day, cheering him on and applauding his good shots. And he made quite a few. As for his chances of winning, he made it clear.

"If I didn't think I could win here, I wouldn't have flown over," he said. "It's quite a long way."

No one, though, thought so highly of his own chances as Mickelson, who came into the Open holding the 2005 PGA Championship and having won his second Masters in April. Nor had anyone in this field prepared so diligently and so thoroughly. He had visited the club often, and, following a Hoganesque program, spent much of the previous week playing the course and working on the shots he would need.

Mickelson had carried two drivers occasionally, one to shape the drive from left to right, the other to shape it right to left, in his case a fade. After his studies he chose to carry only the left-to-right club, the driver with the shorter shaft as well. It worked fairly well. Mickelson hit nine of the 14 fairways on driving holes and eight greens.

He began his round from the 10th tee and struggled to match par on the second nine. He missed every green from the 12th through the 17th, but he saved his even-par 35 with exceptional putting and a marvelous short game. At the 18th, for example, his ninth hole of the round, he holed from 40 feet and birdied.

Mickelson played more steadily on his second nine, yet watched a three-foot putt for a par at the second catch the lip of the hole and spin away. Later he missed a chance to break par by three-putting the fifth hole, at 515 yards, much the shorter of the two par 5s. His first putt died six feet short of the hole, and he missed the second.

Speaking of it later, Mickelson said he wasn't upset, but not overly pleased with his par at the fifth. "I hit a perfect drive, hit a good 7-iron about 50 feet behind the hole, where I wanted it to be, and I didn't hit a good first putt."

Nevertheless, Mickelson stood just one stroke behind the leader, and with three rounds to play he held hope he could add the U.S. Open to his resume.

Then there was 15-year-old Tadd Fujikawa, the youngest golfer ever to play in the championship. Tadd struggled around Winged Foot in 81 strokes and had little hope of playing over the weekend. He hit eight fairways, but considering he had put his ball in play on five more holes than Woods, four more than David Duval, and a few more than Ogilvy, Padraig Harrington and Steve Stricker, he played rather well. And he enjoyed it. Besides, he threw all his 5-foot-1 and 130 pounds into one drive and ripped it 301 yards.

"It was a lot of fun," he said at day's end. "I honestly thought I would be a little more nervous, but after the first shot I started getting a little calmer. It's the U.S. Open, so I better have fun. No matter what I shoot I'll have fun."

Ah, youth.

John Cook (71) posted four birdies.

Tadd Fujikawa (81) enjoyed his first Open.

31

His chances fading, Tiger Woods (152) could gain no ground here at the par-5 fifth (his 14th hole of the day).

In the pecking order of championship golf, Tiger Woods ranks considerably higher than Steve Stricker. And yet it is safe to assume that after two rounds of the U.S. Open, Woods would have been delighted to trade their 36-hole scores. For good reason. Stricker stood at the top of the list with 139 while Woods had fallen 13 strokes behind him and missed the cut.

Here we had a double surprise.

By 2006 Woods brought fear to the heart whenever he stepped onto the tee, while Stricker had become a 39-year-old journeyman. Yet, after two rounds over Winged Foot's punishing West Course, Stricker led this select field and Woods was going home. This was new ground for both: Stricker had never led the Open, and Woods had never failed to play every round except in his first faltering attempt as an amateur in 1995.

The most obvious similarity in their careers was that Stricker's agent was Mark Steinberg, who also represented Woods. A friend since their college days at the University of Illinois, Steinberg had two other golf clients, both ranked No. 1 in the world, Woods and Annika Sorenstam.

After an opening 70, Stricker played Winged Foot in 69 the second day and climbed past Colin Montgomerie into first place. Montgomerie slipped to 71 after his opening 69, and at 140 stood one stroke ahead of Geoff Ogilvy and Kenneth Ferrie. Both Ogilvy and Ferrie had scores of 71 and 70. A stroke behind, tied for fifth place at 142, Jim Furyk shot 72 and Padraig Harrington 69.

Phil Mickelson had followed his opening 70 with 73 and dropped into a tie for seventh with Arron Oberholser, who had won at Pebble Beach early in the year, Jason Dufner, playing in his second Open, and the Irishman Graeme McDowell, all unfamiliar names.

Overall, five men broke par: Oberholser and David Duval with 68, and Stricker, Harrington and Luke Donald, who shot 69.

Starting from the 10th tee six strokes behind the leader, Duval revived the skills of his earlier years, played the second nine in 33 strokes, the first nine in 35, and leaped 76 places, from a tie for 90th into a tie for 14th.

Both Tom Pernice and Tommy Armour III, meanwhile, saved themselves from elimination with even-par 70s that offset their 79s in the first round. But then Kevin Stadler played the first round in 71, then ruined his week by slipping to 81 in the second.

Gallery members absorbed all this, but most eyes focused not on the leaders and the low scores but on the 36-hole cut that would trim the field to the low 60 players and any tied for 60th place. They speculated on whether Woods would survive to play the last two rounds. He had played in 10 consecutive Opens and had never missed the final two rounds, but he had begun the second round in danger of ruining that record. And indeed he did, missing the cut in a major championship for the first time as a professional. Including his last two as an amateur, Woods had survived 39 consecutive cuts before this.

With two scores of 76, he missed by three strokes.

After his first round of 75, Michael Campbell, the 2005 champion, began the second round from the 10th tee and played a reasonable 36, but he

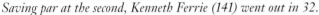

Saving par at the second, Kenneth Ferrie (141) went out in 32.

Graeme McDowell (143) did not putt well.

Jason Dufner (143) 'tried to stay patient.'

A year earlier Allen Doyle had shot 63 in the final round of the U.S. Senior Open, passed nine others, and won the championship. He had no such golf in him at Winged Foot. Two weeks short of his 58th birthday, Doyle, a bulky 6-foot-3, turned in rounds of 76 and 74 and missed by just one stroke. Of his last five holes, he bogeyed three and birdied two. Together with two others, Doyle birdied twice as many holes as Woods.

Woods had had a good run in the Open. He had first played in 1995, and had injured his wrist tearing his ball from the rough along the sixth hole at Shinnecock Hills and had withdrawn during the second round. He was 19 years old at the time, still in college.

bogeyed seven holes on the first nine, came back in 41, shot 77 and missed with 152, the same score as Woods, playing in the same group with U.S. Amateur champion Edoardo Molinari, who shot one stroke worse.

Retief Goosen had not been the same after his miserable 81 in the final round at Pinehurst a year earlier, and here he played two dreary rounds of 77 and 78. Sergio Garcia, still in search of his first major, played one stroke worse, and Davis Love III, perhaps trying to catch the magic of his 1997 PGA Championship over this same course, shot 154 and missed the cut as well.

He began his 10-year string of making cuts at Oakland Hills the following year. He had tied for the lead at three under par midway through the first round, but it all fell apart at the 16th. Trying to clear a pond, his ball struck a rock and bounded into the water, he made an 8, four strokes above the hole's par, shot 76, and finished far down the standings with 294. Still, he beat Mickelson by two strokes.

No single hole bedeviled him at Winged Foot. He simply failed to control his shots. Where he found the fairway with only three drives in the

Second Round

Steve Stricker	70 – 69	– 139	-1
Colin Montgomerie	69 – 71	– 140	E
Geoff Ogilvy	71 – 70	– 141	+1
Kenneth Ferrie	71 – 70	– 141	+1
Jim Furyk	70 – 72	– 142	+2
Padraig Harrington	73 – 69	– 142	+2
Graeme McDowell	71 – 72	– 143	+3
Phil Mickelson	70 – 73	– 143	+3
Arron Oberholser	75 – 68	– 143	+3
Jason Dufner	72 – 71	– 143	+3
Scott Hend	72 – 72	– 144	+4
Bart Bryant	72 – 72	– 144	+4
Phillip Archer	72 – 72	– 144	+4

Geoff Ogilvy (141) said his start was 'pretty nice.'

first round, he hit four in the second, but while he reached 10 greens with the appropriate shot in the first round, he hit only eight in the second. Clearly, he would not win a prize for his putting, and his ball-striking was far below his usual standard.

Winged Foot's 16th hole is no pushover. It measures 478 yards with a sharp dogleg to the left, but its green lies wide open. Since Woods started from the 10th tee, he played the 16th as his seventh of the day. He found the fairway for a change, and with a clear shot into the green, he yanked his ball so far left it hit a tree, ricocheted onto a cart path and jumped into a bunker protecting the 12th green of Winged Foot's East Course.

When the turmoil ended he had his second double bogey of the day. He made his first two holes earlier at the 14th, another dogleg left. He missed the green, played a poor chip, then missed a two-foot putt for the bogey.

A birdie at the 17th gave him hope, and he ran off four consecutive pars. His chance to survive ended at the fourth hole. From mid-fairway he played an iron that so disgusted him that with the ball still airborne he dropped his club over his shoulder and turned his back. He had left himself a 60-foot putt. He three-putted. Sadly, that was a bogey he couldn't afford. He closed his round with two more, shot another 76, then headed for home.

Arron Oberholser (143) shot 68 despite a bogey at No. 18.

With a birdie from the bunker at No. 9 (his 18th), Steve Stricker (139) celebrated his 69 with caddie Tom Mitchell.

"I'm more frustrated than anything else," Woods claimed, "because I was hitting the ball really well. I didn't execute properly today. I didn't drive the ball well, didn't hit my irons well and didn't have the green speed again. So, not a good combo."

Learning that Woods had missed the cut didn't exactly upset the other players. Speaking honestly, Montgomerie said, "It helps us all. It would be nice to take advantage of his absence."

Others speculated the effect of Woods's performance might possibly influence how others played. It did not influence Stricker. Woods had teed off in the afternoon while Stricker had begun at 7 a.m., the first man off the 10th tee, grouped with Tommy Armour III and Oliver Wilson, an Englishman.

Once again the morning shone bright and clear and the greens were clean and smooth. Since no one had yet played the course, they would never run better. Stricker had played the first nine in 32 strokes in the opening round, and once again he birdied early, holing a 15-foot putt at the 14th, his fifth hole of the round.

He gave the stroke away at the 15th, then took it back by birdieing the difficult 18th, then turned for home one under par. In two days he had played Winged Foot's second nine four under par. Now one under par for 27 holes, he had tied Montgomerie, the first-round leader, still hours away from his 1:58 p.m. starting time.

Moving on to his second nine, Stricker looked as if he might drop a stroke when he bunkered his approach to the second, but drawing his wedge, Stricker pitched into the hole. A birdie 3 where a 5 looked possible, and he had slipped two under par for the round.

Then his game deserted him. Bogeys at the seventh and eighth holes wiped out his two birdies, and it looked worse at the ninth where once again an approach dived into a bunker. Not to worry, for obviously Stricker carried enchanted clubs. With the prospect of finishing with three consecutive bogeys, once again he pitched into the hole for another birdie.

He played the second nine in even-par 35, shot 69, and with 139 for 36 holes he could spend the rest of the day waiting for someone to catch him.

Stricker called his holing out from the bunker a bonus. "I mean I could have bogeyed just as easily, probably," he said, "and been sitting here at one over."

Stricker was no rookie in the Open, he had tied for fifth in both the 1998 Open, at Olympic Club,

Scott Hend (144) said he putted conservatively.

where Lee Janzen won his second, and was fifth alone at Pinehurst the following year, where Payne Stewart won his second. In 1998 he went into the PGA Championship's final round tied with Vijay Singh, but Singh closed with 68 and Stricker with 70 and he lost by two strokes.

Once a fixture on the PGA Tour, Stricker's game had fallen into disrepair. He no longer challenged to win at this level and lost his Tour eligibility by dropping to 151st on the 2004 money list. He had won nothing since the 2001 Match Play Championship, and now he led the game's most important competition. His was a fragile lead, though, for neither Montgomerie nor Mickelson had begun their second round.

Born June 16, 1970, Mickelson was observing his 36th birthday when he stepped onto Winged Foot's first tee that afternoon. It didn't appear to be a happy birthday, though, when he missed both the fairways and the greens of the first two holes and

Phil Mickelson (143) parred No. 15 from the rough.

lost strokes on both. He settled down over the next few holes, hitting fairways and greens and making his figures, but he dropped another stroke at the ninth, again missing fairway, green and a saving putt.

Out in 38, he continued his loose driving, hitting just two of the seven fairways, but he ran in a 30-foot putt and birdied the 13th, drawing a noisy response from his gallery, and he saved his par at the 17th with another of his uncanny bunker shots, this one to less than a foot from the hole.

He played the 18th badly. Choosing to play his

Padraig Harrington (142) birdied No. 18 for his 69.

Jim Furyk (142) reacts to a missed putt at No. 14.

Phillip Archer (144) birdied two of the last four holes.

driver, which had failed him repeatedly through the day, he misplayed the shot and flew it into the left rough. Intent on reaching the green, he attempted a dangerous shot over a towering sugar maple tree. The shot misfired. Instead of the green, it hit a tree branch and dropped straight down.

Mickelson said later the shot should have worked.

"The ball should have jumped over the tree. No problem." But, he said, he hit the shot badly.

Nevertheless, he bogeyed, came back in 35, scored 73 and dropped into a tie for seventh behind, among others, Jim Furyk, the 2003 Open champion.

Furyk had recovered from a weird injury that affected him so badly he withdrew from the previous week's tournament at Westchester. Hunched over a bathroom sink, he suddenly threw his head back to take a pill, then felt the muscles tighten on the left side of his back.

"I probably pinched something in my lower neck or upper back," he said, "and it was difficult to turn my head to the left."

While he had missed the warm-up tournament, nevertheless he played his first round of the Open in even-par 70 and added 72 in the second. At 142, he sat three strokes behind Stricker.

Furyk had dropped to seventh place, but Mont-

Luke Donald (147) shot 69, rising from 112th place.

Colin Montgomerie (140) missed a putt to share the lead.

gomerie lurked just one stroke behind Stricker, and had been playing exceptionally well. The previous July he had finished second to Woods in the British Open, and for a time looked as if he might catch him over the final holes at St. Andrews. Monty had played the first 10 holes of the final round in three under par and climbed within one stroke, but he overshot the 11th green and lost one stroke. He played the home nine in 39, Woods played it in 36 and beat Montgomerie by four strokes. Monty had, however, played strong golf when it mattered.

Going into the second round at Winged Foot protecting first place, Montgomerie played an exceptional round if only for its monotony. He scored pars on 17 of the 18 holes and dropped one stroke at the 14th, a sturdy 458-yard par 4 that had drawn so much blood it ranked below only the first in difficulty. He played a fine drive right of the fairway bunker, then blocked his 6-iron recovery and missed the green to the right. The ball ran down a grade, but Monty played a nice pitch within six feet of a hole tucked in the back left portion of the green, then missed the putt.

Coming in he had birdie openings at the seventh, at 162 yards about the easiest par on the course, and the ninth. He missed a makeable putt at the seventh, and his 20-foot putt at the ninth glided past the hole with little space to spare.

As his ball failed to drop, Montgomerie showed his first hint of pique, but recovered quickly and spoke philosophically.

"That's all I can do," he shrugged. "If I can hang in there the way I did today and have a chance on Sunday...One never knows."

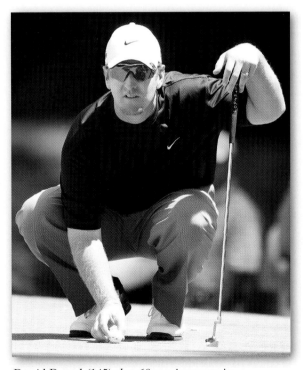

David Duval (145) shot 68 to stir memories.

An enthusiastic crowd cheered his birdie at No. 16, and Phil Mickelson (212) shot 69 to share the lead.

With Tiger Woods, the dominant player of the current century, on his way home, the 63 survivors of the U.S. Open's first two rounds focused instead on Phil Mickelson. Often an afterthought in this championship, Mickelson rose to a first-place tie by playing Winged Foot's second nine in 33 strokes, following a struggling 36 on the outward nine. He came in with 69, one under par, and while he passed five others, he could not shake the Englishman Kenneth Ferrie. Both men had played 54 holes in 212 strokes, two over par.

This was a day as well when Colin Montgomerie recovered from a disheartening start, when Ferrie and Geoff Ogilvy confirmed they could play at this level, when Vijay Singh made a move, when Steve Stricker lost control of his driver and dropped from first place into a tie for fourth, and when David Duval's re-emergence shifted into reverse with his disappointing 75.

Once again Winged Foot asserted itself, if a golf course can. Aside from Mickelson, only Ryuji Imada broke par by matching Mickelson's 69, and just five others shot 70. Imada, by the way, had tied for 15th at Pinehurst a year earlier.

Ferrie claimed his share of the lead with his second 71, and he could have taken first place alone if not for a bogey 5 at the 18th. For someone in his first U.S. Open, he had played remarkably steady golf. Of course he had lost two strokes to par on both the 14th and 15th holes in the second round, but he had shrugged them off, played the last three holes in even par and shot 70.

Ogilvy came in with 72 and moved into third place at 213, just one stroke off the lead, and both

Singh and Ian Poulter, he of the raucous wardrobe, shot 70 and shared fourth place at 215 with Montgomerie and Stricker, who dropped four shots in the last six holes.

Jim Furyk, Mike Weir and Padraig Harrington lurked another stroke back at 216 with just one round to play. All three stumbled at the end. Furyk bogeyed two of the last three holes, Weir took a double-bogey 6 at the 18th, and Harrington finished with a triple-bogey 7.

Once again the gallery cheered Mickelson's every movement, especially as he played the last six holes in 21 strokes, a stretch when he demonstrated precision driving and deadly putting.

With only a mild wind, the temperature turned slightly uncomfortable, but the gallery members didn't seem to mind. About 35,000 poured through the entranceways, the largest of the week so far. Some followed a particular player, others sought special places where they could watch the passing parade of the game's leading players. Those who chose to watch the third hole witnessed the most spectacular shot of the week.

Six over par after 38 holes, Peter Hedblom, a blond, 36-year-old Swede, stood on the third tee and stared at a green with a narrow opening and the hole set close to its narrowest point. Hedblom drew a 3-iron and ripped into a shot that flew directly at the flagstick. The ball came to ground short of the green, took a few bounces and rolled into the hole. Hedblom had scored a hole-in-one at the longest par 3 in memory. Normally a 216-yard par 3, it had been stretched to 243 yards for the third round.

When the ball fell from sight, Hedblom's jaw dropped, his grin widened and he shared high-fives

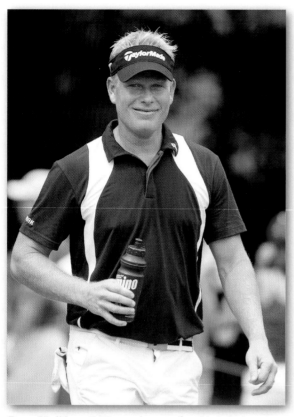

Peter Hedblom (217) was happy after his hole-in-one.

Mike Weir (216) shot 71 with a 6 at No. 18.

Third Round

Phil Mickelson	70 - 73 - 69 – 212	+2
Kenneth Ferrie	71 - 70 - 71 – 212	+2
Geoff Ogilvy	71 - 70 - 72 – 213	+3
Ian Poulter	74 - 71 - 70 – 215	+5
Vijay Singh	71 - 74 - 70 – 215	+5
Colin Montgomerie	69 - 71 - 75 – 215	+5
Steve Stricker	70 - 69 - 76 – 215	+5
Mike Weir	71 - 74 - 71 – 216	+6
Padraig Harrington	73 - 69 - 74 – 216	+6
Jim Furyk	70 - 72 - 74 – 216	+6
Trevor Immelman	76 - 71 - 70 – 217	+7
Luke Donald	78 - 69 - 70 – 217	+7
Peter Hedblom	72 - 74 - 71 – 217	+7
Bart Bryant	72 - 72 - 73 – 217	+7
Arron Oberholser	75 - 68 - 74 – 217	+7

with Stewart Cink, his pairing mate, and their caddies. With that shot he dropped to four under par. Two holes later, playing the fifth, at 515 yards a pushover par 5, Hedblom played a nice drive and followed with a 5-wood to about 20 feet and holed the putt for an eagle 3. Now he stood just three strokes out of first place.

Of course it didn't last. He bogeyed the ninth, played the homeward nine in 39, and with a round of 71, tied for 11th place.

Playing the game as he hadn't in some years, Steve Stricker had climbed to the top with a second-round 69, and he would leave the first tee in the last pairing of the third round, along with Montgomerie, not enjoying this day nearly as well as the previous two.

Driving well at the beginning, Stricker ran off four pars, then scored a birdie at the par-5 fifth by reaching the green with his second shot and getting down in two putts. Suddenly, though, his game deserted him. He missed both the fairway and the green of the sixth, the 321-yard par 4, and dropped one stroke, then lost two more at the eighth and ninth. He went out in 37.

Stricker's driving had been exceptional considering the narrow width of Winged Foot's fairways. He had placed his drives on 23 of 32 fairways

Steve Stricker (215) struggled to find the fairway and fell from first to a tie for fourth place.

through the fifth hole of the third round, but then he lost control and played a series of pull hooks. His drive at the eighth flew deep into the rough and he bogeyed, then he lost another stroke at the ninth, where his long downhill putt ran miles past the hole.

His first nine had been bad enough, but he played the second nine worse. Stricker had owned that second nine through the first two rounds. He had shot 32 in the opening round and 34 in the second. Now, though, he played a series of holes highlighted by the 14th, a demanding par 4 with a decided swing to the left in the drive zone. Throwing some extra muscle into his drive, he pulled his ball so far left and into such deep rough he couldn't hack it to the fairway. He lashed into the shot with all he could give, but the ball rose barely above his knees. It did, however, maneuver to shorter grass, but when he finally holed out he had lost two more strokes. From one under par after five holes, he had fallen to four over with four holes to play.

Two more bogeys and he finished the second

Vijay Singh (215) stayed in contention with 70, even par.

43

Including here at the third, Colin Montgomerie (215) took bogeys on the first four holes, but settled down for a 75.

Arron Oberholser (217) bounced from 75 to 68 to 74.

nine in 39 strokes, returned a score of 76, and fell from first place into a tie for fourth.

Looking back, Stricker realized his problems went deeper than his driving. His putting let him down as well. "I just couldn't get anything to go in," he said. Then turning to his driving, he added, "I hit a couple of quick pulls and struggled to get on the fairway. Around here if you're struggling to get in the fairway, you're in deep trouble."

Stricker had company. Through two days of steady golf, an accomplishment over this punishing course, Montgomerie had gone over par on just four holes. Suddenly he lost his touch and dropped four strokes over the first four of the third round and added another at the sixth, the short but dangerous par 4. He did, however, birdie the vulnerable fifth and went out in an undignified 40 strokes.

Montgomerie had settled down by the seventh and played the remaining 12 holes in even par, birdieing the 14th, which had so perplexed Stricker, and dropping a stroke at the 16th. That hole had surrendered just 39 birdies, but it claimed 147 scores

Former Mayor Rudolph Giuliani watched with his wife.

over its par of 4. Montgomerie came back in 35 and dropped three strokes behind the leaders.

Commenting on his day, Monty described his opening holes as a disaster, and with a touch of sarcasm said, "Five over after four holes is just what you're looking for, you know.

"After half an hour I'm down from second spot to 15th. But then level par in, I got myself up into fourth spot, and there are only three guys ahead of me. Around here, if I can drive the ball the way I know I can, and the way I finished, I'll be okay."

Not many fans had followed Ogilvy's progress, although he had played rock steady golf, turning in 71 and 70 the first two days, then 72 in the third round.

Fairly new to the United States, he had played in the 2003 and 2005 Opens, missed the cut in 2003 and tied for 26th place in 2005. He had, however, played in a number of PGA Tour events, and had won the Match Play Championship in February. He did it the hard way. His first four matches went to extra holes, but then he brought in Tom Lehman 4 and 3 in a semifinal, and Davis Love III, 3 and 2, in the final match. Two weeks later he came in second in the Honda Classic, in Florida, but he had placed among the leading 10 scorers only once in the other 12 events he had entered.

Nevertheless, hardly anyone had noticed his fair amount of success. Simply put, Ogilvy lacked the flair of the Montgomeries, the Mickelsons and

Padraig Harrington (216) dropped with a 7 at the 18th.

Geoff Ogilvy (213) let his clubs speak for him.

Fred Couples (218) shot 71 and moved into the top 20.

Kenneth Ferrie (212) was standing out in his first Open.

the Ferries. He dressed conservatively and spoke quietly. With none of the flaming temper of Montgomerie in his earlier days, or the boyishly shy grin of Mickelson, Ogilvy walked by hardly noticed. Until one watched him play.

Tall, at 6-foot-2 and a sturdy 180 pounds, he could outdrive much of the Open field, and he largely avoided the kind of dangerous shots that often ruin those who don't. Strategy such as this may not attract the galleries, but it wins tournaments.

Off to a shaky start with a 5 at the first hole, a not uncommon number, Ogilvy steadied ship and ran off eight consecutive pars. And he was unlucky not to have birdied the ninth. His putt from 40 feet to a hole set in the green's lower right corner looked ready to fall, but it missed by the barest margin. Minutes later, with the hole of the 10th tucked once more in the green's lower right, Ogilvy made his birdie 2. Even par now, he misplayed both the 13th and 14th and completed his round with four immaculate 4s on the closing holes.

Trevor Immelman (217) finished with six pars.

Ian Poulter (215) shot 70, but ended with a 6.

Playing alongside him, Ferrie attracted most of the gallery's attention. A bulky Englishman, at 6-foot-4 he stood two inches taller than Ogilvy and many pounds heavier. Not long before he arrived at Winged Foot he weighed 280 pounds, but by Open time he had shed 50 or so pounds, not exactly slim, but hardly obese.

Ferrie hailed from Ashington, in northeastern England, near Newcastle, and appeared to have an easygoing if eccentric personality. He arrived for the third round with his pants held up by a white belt bearing the Superman emblem. It caught everyone's attention. He favored tight, light gray slacks that hung low on the hips.

David Duval (220) dropped back with 75.

Jim Furyk (216) and caddie Mike (Fluff) Cowen study a Winged Foot green while posting a 74 in the third round.

Adam Scott (218) hit 15 greens and shot 70.

His kept hair short and dark, he bedecked his chin with a goatee, and he wore a white visor that he whipped on and off as the tension rose and fell. And for someone in his first Open at the age of 27, he played a quality game of golf, breezing around Winged Foot in 34-37–71, passing Ogilvy and climbing from a tie for third place into a tie for first.

A crowd-pleaser Ferrie may be, but the hearts of the gallery belonged to Mickelson. Right-handed by nature but left-handed on the golf course, Mickelson had graduated from Arizona State University in 1992 with impressive credentials, most prominently as a U.S. Amateur champion and then a member of two Walker Cup teams and one United States team in the World Amateur Team Championship as well.

Success did not come so easily when he turned to professional golf. He won a number of the regular PGA Tour events, but he played for years before winning one of the significant tournaments that mean so much to a player's prestige. Finally he won the 2004 Masters Tournament, repeated in 2006

START	LEADERS	1	2	3	4	5	6	7	8	9	10	11	12	13	14	15	16	17	18	RD 1	RD 2	RD 3	RD 4
	PAR	4	4	3	4	5	4	3	4	4	3	4	5	3	4	4	4	4	4				
1	STRICKER					2				0						3	3			70	69		
0	MONTGOMERIE	1	2	4	5	4	5	5	5	5	5	5	5	5	4	4				69	71		
1	FERRIE	1	1	0	1	1	1	1	1	1	0	0	0	0	1	1	1	1		71	70		
1	OGILVY	2	2	2	2	2	2	2	2	1	1	1	2	3	3	3				71	70		
3	MCDOWELL	2	2	2	1	1	2	2	3	3	3	3	4	5	5	6	6			71	72		
5	SINGH V	5	5	5	4	3	3	4	4	5	4	4	5	5	5	5	5	5		71	74	70	
2	HARRINGTON	2	1	2	2	2	1	1	1	2	2	2	2	3	2	3	3			73	69		
5	POULTER	5	5	5	5	3	3	3	4	3	3	3	3	4	3	3	3	5		74	71	70	
3	MICKELSON	3	3	4	3	3	2	2	3	4	4	4	4	4	3	3	2	2		70	73		
2	FURYK	2	2	2	2	2	3	3	3	5	5	5	5	5	4	5				70	72		

Mickelson found his name next to the bottom, but tied for the lead after Ferrie took a bogey at the 18th.

and won the 2005 PGA Championship. Three times he placed second in the Open, first to Payne Stewart at Pinehurst in 1999, then to Tiger Woods at Bethpage in 2002, and most recently to Retief Goosen at Shinnecock Hills in 2004.

Often an erratic driver but blessed with a sometimes uncanny short game, Mickelson had devoted a great amount of time and effort to the Open, and the time had come to collect.

At first this didn't look to be Mickelson's day. Through the first nine he missed all but two fairways and four greens, lost one stroke at the third hole, one of the longest par 3s in any U.S. Open, took it back with a birdie at the fourth, and added another at the sixth, a short par 4 with a bunker set along the left side.

A extraordinary bunker player, Mickelson determined that as a part of his strategy he would aim his tee shot for that bunker. As planned, he hit the target and then stunned the gallery with a pitch with an almost flat 64-degree wedge that landed softly and settled a little more than a foot from the hole. He birdied and went one under for the day.

He lost those strokes quickly with bogeys at the eighth and ninth holes, and continued missing fairways on the early holes of the second nine.

As Rick Smith, Mickelson's swing coach, described it, something suddenly clicked and he couldn't miss. He hit every fairway starting with the 14th and every green from the 11th, played an especially good drive that split the fairway of the 18th, birdied both the 14th and 16th, which together surrendered only 13 birdies during the round, came back in 33 and with 69 joined Ferrie at the top of the list.

Asked later if it would be looking ahead to ask what winning the U.S. Open would mean to him, Mickelson suggested it certainly would be looking ahead. Then he added:

"Let's just wait another 24 hours and see if I put together one more good round."

The only birdies of the day for Geoff Ogilvy (285) came at No. 5 and here at No. 6, where he pitched and one-putted.

106th
U.S. OPEN
Fourth Round

Many championships have been lost in the past because of poorly played shots at vital moments, or foolish decisions where clear thinking could have made the difference between winning or losing. Rarely, though, has a championship been lost with so much previous warning as Phil Mickelson's butchering of the 18th hole at Winged Foot in the final round of the U.S. Open.

Needing just a bogey 5 to tie, Mickelson, playing in the last pairing of the day, ripped into a drive and pushed it so far left it hit the roof of a huge hospitality tent and bounced back toward the fairway into dead grass worn out by spectator traffic. He had pushed the shot so far left his ball lay beyond the tallest rough.

He had a serious problem, though. A towering maple tree blocked his line to the green, the same tree that cost him a stroke in the second round. He had visions then of carrying a shot over the tree, but the ball hit a branch and dropped straight down. He did manage to lose just one stroke then, but here his ball lay in the heavy rough. The U.S. Open was Mickelson's to win or lose. At four over par with only the last hole to play, he could win with a par 4, and with a bogey 5 he could force a playoff with Geoff Ogilvy, who, playing directly ahead of him, had finished with 72 for a 285 total, five strokes over par.

Mickelson chose to gamble, tried a risky shot that, if it worked, would turn from right to left around the tree and perhaps onto the green. Once again it failed. Instead of clearing the tree, it struck it headlong. The ball caromed back no more than 30 feet from where his drive had lain. Instead of a

possible 4, he would struggle to make the bogey and catch Ogilvy.

Mickelson made a 6, for a round of 74 and a 286 total, and Ogilvy became the U.S. Open champion. That left Mickelson tied for second place with Jim Furyk, who shot 70, and Colin Montgomerie, who finished with 71.

A deflated Mickelson, stunned by what he had done, muttered, "I can't believe I did that." With that one risky shot he wrecked a week of first-class golf and earned his finish a place among the memorable collapses of championship golf.

Among them:

1999: Three strokes ahead standing on the 18th tee at Carnoustie in the British Open, Jean Van de Velde played a wild drive into a good lie well off the fairway about 190 yards from the green. With the option of playing a safe shot back to the fairway and then pitching on, or going for the green, he went for the green, played a loose 2-iron that by a fluke hit the railing of a grandstand and carried back across the Barry Burn into impossible rough. From there he chopped his ball into the burn, played the hole in seven strokes, and lost a playoff to Paul Lawrie.

1939: Needing only a par 5 but believing he must birdie to win the U.S. Open at Philadelphia Country Club's Spring Mill Course, Sam Snead hooked his drive into rough grass, topped a 2-wood and ran it into a steep-faced bunker, left it there trying to escape with an 8-iron and instead embedded the ball in the seams of freshly laid sod, chopped it out into another bunker, played his fifth shot onto the green but 40 feet from the hole, three-putted for an 8, and dropped to fourth place, two strokes

Ian Poulter (289) leaps to follow his shot from the rough.

Jeff Sluman (288) went out in 32, low for the week.

Nick O'Hern (288) posted 69 to tie for sixth.

behind Byron Nelson, Craig Wood and Denny Shute. Nelson won the playoff.

1920: With a strong wind whipping directly against him, Harry Vardon tried to reach the 17th green at Inverness Club with his 2-wood and salvage the U.S. Open Championship. Two 4s would do it, but his shot had to carry a brook running across the fairway directly in front of the green. His ball cleared the near bank, but it slammed into the far bank and dropped into the brook. Vardon tied for second, one stroke behind Ted Ray, a fellow Englishman.

1932: At a period when the PGA of America conducted its championship at match play, Al Watrous stood 9-up after the 22nd hole of a 36-hole match with Bobby Cruickshank. If Cruickshank missed his six-foot putt, he would fall to 10-down, but taking pity, Watrous conceded the putt and the half. A grave mistake. Cruickshank won nine of the next 11 holes, took the match to extra holes, and won when Watrous missed a three-foot putt at the 41st.

Some critics will mention Arnold Palmer in 1966 at The Olympic Club. Palmer led by seven strokes standing on the 10th tee, but Billy Casper caught him and won the Open in a playoff the next day. We should not forget, though, that while Palmer did indeed drop four strokes over par that final nine, at the same time Casper played them in 32, three under par.

There have been others, but those will do. After the debacle, popular attention settled around Mickelson, but while it made no difference to him, his was not the only failure at the 18th hole.

Playing four groups ahead of Mickelson, Furyk came to the final hole at five over par and bogeyed. Two groups later Montgomerie stepped onto the 18th tee just four over par, played a good drive, then under-clubbed his approach, had nothing but a chip to the green, then three-putted for a 6 to finish six over.

As late as the 16th tee, Padraig Harrington could have finished at four over par, but he lost strokes on each of the last three holes for a 71 and fell to fifth place, at 287, two strokes too many.

Once again the field played under sunny skies and fair weather and watched by another large gallery. Spectators lined every fairway, sometimes pushing against the restraining ropes to follow a shot, then moving on for the next. Those alert enough picked up Jeff Sluman as he whipped through the first nine in 32 strokes, matching the low nine-hole score of the week, or David Duval, who bounced back from his 75 the previous day with a closing 71 that lifted him into a tie for 16th place, a heady level for him lately.

At 5-foot-7 and 140 pounds, Sluman gives hope to the undersized among us because he has played championship golf for 25 years and still can compete at that level. He had placed second by two strokes to Tom Kite in 1992, playing the third round at Pebble Beach in 69 strokes. He bettered Montgomerie, who placed third, by one stroke.

Coming in, Sluman lost strokes at the 10th and 16th, but where others foundered, Sluman hit the fairway of the 18th, hit the green and got down in two putts. Could he have sold that finish, the takers would have lined up.

Duval, meanwhile, began his day by birdieing the first hole, as tough a hole as the 18th, and going

Paul Casey (290) had one of the four 69s.

53

Phil Mickelson (286) birdied No. 14 to take the lead.

Ryuji Imada (289) finished with three bogeys.

Fourth Round

Geoff Ogilvy	71 - 70 - 72 - 72 – 285	+5
Jim Furyk	70 - 72 - 74 - 70 – 286	+6
Colin Montgomerie	69 - 71 - 75 - 71 – 286	+6
Phil Mickelson	70 - 73 - 69 - 74 – 286	+6
Padraig Harrington	73 - 69 - 74 - 71 – 287	+7
Nick O'Hern	75 - 70 - 74 - 69 – 288	+8
Jeff Sluman	74 - 73 - 72 - 69 – 288	+8
Mike Weir	71 - 74 - 71 - 72 – 288	+8
Steve Stricker	70 - 69 - 76 - 73 – 288	+8
Vijay Singh	71 - 74 - 70 - 73 – 288	+8
Kenneth Ferrie	71 - 70 - 71 - 76 – 288	+8
Ryuji Imada	76 - 73 - 69 - 71 – 289	+9
Luke Donald	78 - 69 - 70 - 72 – 289	+9
Ian Poulter	74 - 71 - 70 - 74 – 289	+9
Paul Casey	77 - 72 - 72 - 69 – 290	+10

out in 34. One under par for the day, he played erratic golf coming in, three-putting the 10th, regaining that stroke with his second consecutive birdie at the 11th, then losing two strokes and coming in with 37.

Sluman had begun tied for 20th place and Duval tied for 32nd, but at the end of the day Sluman had climbed into a tie for sixth and Duval to a 16th-place tie, and, more importantly, suggested he had returned to his earlier form.

Still, they played no role in deciding the championship. Those who would teed off behind them. Of those, Furyk and Harrington teed off first, just ahead of Steve Stricker and Mike Weir. Stricker began the day tied for fourth place. He hadn't been this close to first place in some years, and he wouldn't finish there. Playing inconsistent golf, Stricker parred just one-third of the holes, birdied three, eagled one, bogeyed the rest, shot 73 for the day, 288 for the championship, and dropped into a tie for sixth alongside, among others, Kenneth Ferrie, who played his weakest golf of the week.

His disappointing performance puzzled Ferrie because he had such confidence he held an inner feeling he could win, stating, "I had a suspicion that maybe today was meant to be my day."

He certainly began as if it very well could by

Vijay Singh (288) saved par here at the second, but his 73 included five bogeys.

running off six consecutive pars. Just then the mood changed, along with his control of his putter, and he bogeyed four of the next five holes, three-putting the seventh and eighth and missing the greens of the 10th and 11th. Two more bogeys and he shot 76 for the day, five strokes above his poorest golf of the first three rounds. He simply had no more to give, but he regretted nothing.

"I'll wake up tomorrow, and I'm sure I'll be really pleased with what I've done this week," he said, but the championship would be decided by five others.

Paired together, Furyk and Harrington left the first tee 40 minutes ahead of Mickelson and four strokes behind him. Before the round ended, each man would have his opportunity to win the Open. Within five holes, Furyk had cut his deficit to two by birdieing the first hole, one of just 18 birdies it surrendered through the week, and the fifth hole, which, by contrast, gave up 174.

Those strokes vanished with lost strokes at the seventh and ninth, but he played the first eight

Kenneth Ferrie (288) made his fourth bogey at the 11th.

55

Jim Furyk (286) shot 70 with a bogey at 18.

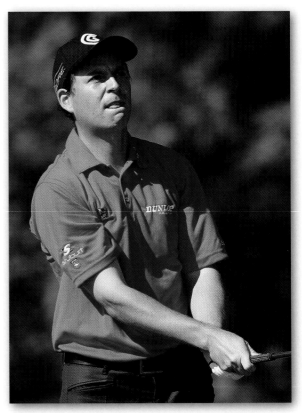

David Howell (291) shot 69 to tie for 16th place.

Padraig Harrington (287) dropped shots at the last three.

holes of the second nine one under par. With the opportunity to finish at five over par, Furyk missed a par putt from no more than four feet at the 18th and settled on even-par 70 for the day and 286 for the 72 holes.

As so many others, Harrington had his opening as well. A Dubliner, he stands a little above 6 feet, walks with an unusual gate, rocking his shoulders from side to side, and stands up to a putt with his legs spread wide apart. He placed high in two U.S. Opens, tying for fifth at Pebble Beach in 2000 and for eighth at Bethpage in 2002. In his best showings in the United States in 2006, he tied for fifth in the Match Play Championship and tied for 11th in New Orleans a few weeks before the Open. He played the first 15 holes of the final round at Winged Foot in two under par. With three more pars he would shoot 284, which in the end would have won the championship, but instead he missed all three greens and fell to 287.

Eventually the Open would come down to

Colin Montgomerie (286) saved par from a bunker at No. 11, and trailed by one stroke at that time.

three men — Montgomerie, Ogilvy and Mickelson, in that order.

This was Montgomerie's 14th U.S. Open. Twice he had placed second, first at Oakmont in 1994, losing a playoff to Ernie Els, and in 1997, again to Els. He had come in third in his first U.S. Open, at Pebble Beach in 1992, the year Tom Kite took the championship.

Here at Winged Foot he had begun the final round at five over par and whittled it down to three over with an outward 33. Bogeys at the 10th and 14th cost him both of those strokes, and he fell to six over through the 16th. Then a birdie at the 17th boosted him back into the hunt with only the trying 18th ahead.

Montgomerie played an excellent drive to the fairway. A bulky man with a ground-eating stride, he lumbered to his ball, then waited while the players up ahead holed out. Finally ready to play, Mont-

Luke Donald (289) shot 72 and held his place.

Ogilvy negotiated the 17th and here at the 18th safely, and with good fortune, to be in position to win.

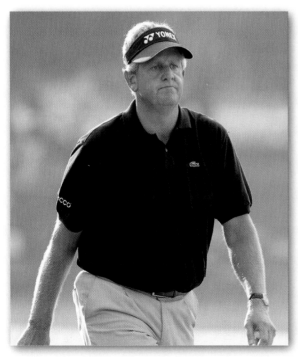

A solemn Montgomerie left the 18th green.

gomerie drew his 6-iron from his bag, gave it some thought, then exchanged it for his 7-iron. He'd made a mistake. As he made contact he seemed to quit on the shot. The ball drifted off to the right as he yelled, "What kind of shot is that!," and dug into menacing rough right of the green.

Now he faced a dangerous shot over a rise onto the green. He popped the ball out, but it ran miles past the hole. He went for the putt but rolled it too far, then missed the next. A 6 on a hole he might have birdied, and rather than the 69 he had within reach, he shot 71 and 286, again one too many.

Ogilvy followed Montgomerie, and for a time at the 17th looked as if he, too, would toss everything away. He pushed his drive so far right into such heavy rough at the 17th he couldn't get to the fairway with his second. He made it with his third and carried the shot into more rough just off the left side of the green. With a stroke of great fortune, he chipped in and saved his par.

Moving to the 18th, Ogilvy's drive down the

Mickelson's third shot from here was partially buried in a bunker, and Phil could not believe what he had done.

center of the fairway rolled into a sand-filled divot, which could have ruined his shot. Instead, he dug it out, the sand exploding from the divot, but the ball came to ground just short of the green, then rolled back down the steep slope. With delicate finesse, he pitched it a yard or so past the hole, then ran it in. He had overcome two unpredictable situations, shot his second consecutive 72, and now waited to see Mickelson finish.

Mickelson found more trouble over those last two holes than Ogilvy. His drive from the 17th tee dived into a trash receptacle so deep that, when he reached in to lift it out, his head disappeared. He salvaged a par 4, then moved on to the 18th.

His driving had been poor throughout the day. Through the 17 holes he had found the fairway just twice, and not once on the second nine. Here he hit the tent, hit the tree and hit the left greenside bunker. His ball partially buried in the sand, Mickelson's recovery ran over the green, he missed the putt coming back, and lost the Open.

As he waited for Ferrie to putt his ball, Mickelson squatted on his haunches, held his putter in his hand and stared at the ground, despairing at what he had done. Safe to say, that moment will haunt him throughout his days.

Ogilvy, with wife Juli, stepped out to claim the trophy.

Geoff Ogilvy was the first Australian champion in the U.S. Open in 25 years, but one of many great Aussie players.

106th
U.S. OPEN
The Champion

Late in the evening, long after Walter Driver, the USGA president, handed him the United States Open trophy, Geoff Ogilvy and a battalion of friends swooped into the bar of his hotel in White Plains, N.Y., still reeling from the thrill of winning the championship. That silver chalice stocked with the appropriate bubbly, as protocol insisted, Ogilvy drank from it and passed it around. Then they switched to bottles of beer. Most were, after all, Australians.

Among them, Adam Scott had watched Ogilvy's finish sitting in Ernie Els's private airplane waiting to take off for London from the Westchester County Airport. The last putt holed, Scott dashed from the airport and sped back to Winged Foot to join the party. At 25, four years younger than Ogilvy, Scott had been thought of as the best young player among the 23 Australians on the PGA Tour. He had been caught, if not replaced.

Ogilvy's winning had been a singular moment for a number of reasons. Twenty-five years after David Graham won the 1981 championship by playing an immaculate final round at Merion Golf Club, Ogilvy became the second U.S. Open champion from Australia.

Contacted for his reaction, Graham was quoted in the USGA press notes as saying, "I think it's fantastic. I think it's wonderful. Being the only member of the club can be a very lonely job, and now there are two of us. I don't know Geoff, but I would like to meet him and welcome him into this very exclusive club.

"A lot of Australians paid their dues and paved the way to Geoff's success, and not just Greg Norman. Players such as Kel Nagle, Bruce Devlin,

Peter Thomson, Norman Von Nida and Eric Cremin, the great Australian players. They should get credit for what Australian golf has become."

Australia has indeed given us a number of outstanding champions. Thomson won five British Opens, a figure bettered only by Harry Vardon's six. The unlucky Norman won two British Opens, lost a playoff to Fuzzy Zoeller at Winged Foot in the 1984 U.S. Open, lost the 1986 PGA Championship when Bob Tway holed from a bunker on the final hole at Inverness, and lost the 1987 Masters to Larry Mize's outrageous chip that ran into the hole of the 11th, the second playoff hole.

Nagle edged Arnold Palmer by one stroke in the 1960 British Open, Graham won the 1979 PGA Championship, Wayne Grady claimed the 1990 PGA Championship, Ian Baker-Finch took the 1991 British Open, Steve Elkington beat Colin Montgomerie in a playoff for the 1995 PGA Championship, and Jim Ferrier beat Chick Harbert in the 1947 PGA's final match.

Ogilvy, then, had joined select company. But then he was born into select company. He is related to the late Sir Angus Ogilvy, the husband of Princess Alexandra, the granddaughter of King George V and cousin to Queen Elizabeth II. More distantly, Ogilvy is said to be related to Robert The Bruce, the legendary Scottish king who defeated the English at Bannockburn in the 14th century and won Scotland's independence.

An impressive family background, to be sure, but it was his father who launched his golf game at the innocent age of 7.

"He gave me a little cut-down golf club," Ogilvy reminisced, "or a little set of golf clubs, and

I guess I showed some interest. We'd go down to the local muni. I'd play every few weeks, whenever he let me. I guess it was fairly apparent early on that I had a pretty strong interest in the game.

"Probably the first 150 games I played I played with him, because if I didn't play with him, I didn't get to play. When you're 8 or 10 years old you just can't walk up and play golf. You have to have someone to play with.

"The first golf I ever played was at Sandringham Golf Course, across the road from Royal Melbourne." Later he took membership in Cheltenham Golf Club, a neighbor to the better-known Victoria Golf Club.

A natural athlete, by 16 he had improved to scratch and advanced to competitive amateur golf. At 21, he became a professional, played most of his golf on the Australasian Tour, and in 1999 earned the title of Rookie of the Year.

At the same time he expanded his reach, entering 20 tournaments on the European Tour in 1999, and 20 more the next season. By 2001 he had joined the PGA Tour full time, and won his first tournament in 2005, beating Mark Calcavecchia in a playoff in Tucson, the second-tier event played the same week as the Match Play Championship.

Ogilvy struggled to control his temperament early in his career. A perfectionist on the course, he expected his every shot to be played perfectly. When they weren't, he would grow furious with himself. Dale Lynch, from the Victoria Institute of Sport, worked with Ogilvy in his younger days and remembers how the thin and lanky teenager expected so much of himself.

Lynch said, "There were certain situations where his competitiveness and will to win got the better of him. He would get too frustrated and angry, and that had a negative effect." Eventually Ogilvy learned control and developed what someone called "an uncommon equanimity."

Whatever the reason, Ogilvy brought a new attitude to the big events, beginning with the 2005 U.S. Open, at Pinehurst. Thinking back on it, he couldn't explain why.

"I don't know," he said. "For some bizarre reason, starting at Pinehurst last year, I've played bet-

ter at majors than I had up to that point. I don't know why. I got more out of my game at Pinehurst than I should have and finished 25th or something." (Actually, he tied for 28th.)

Speaking of why he handled himself better in the more important occasions, he said, "If I'm two over par after five holes on a Tour event, I'm pretty stroppy. Here it hasn't affected me so much, maybe because I know everyone else is struggling. Or that you've got no chance unless you bring your best attitude to the course and be patient."

A month after Pinehurst, he flew over to St. Andrews, birdied three of the last four holes of the last round and tied for fifth in the British Open. "I played really well," he said, "and those three birdies — that's something special. That gave me a lot of confidence.

"At Baltusrol," Ogilvy said, referring to the PGA Championship, "I finished just ahead of Tiger. I was the leader in the clubhouse, and then he birdied the last hole to get one in front of me." He tied for fifth place, three strokes behind Phil Mickelson, who won the championship.

Ogilvy won his second PGA Tour event early in 2006, beating Davis Love III in the final match of the Match Play Championship, then placed second in his next tournament and tied for 16th in the Masters. His Open prize money had pushed his 2006 earnings to nearly $4 million, second only to Mickelson. He had indeed developed into one of the game's budding figures.

Meanwhile, Ogilvy had settled into a comfortable life in the United States. Not cutting his ties to Melbourne, his home, Ogilvy had married an American girl, an outgoing former chef from Texas. Juli and Geoff Ogilvy made a home for themselves in Scottsdale, Ariz., a town where Geoff can unwind by playing his string guitar and riding his bicycle through the neighborhoods. The couple expected their first-born late in 2006.

Not the most accurate of drivers, Ogilvy said he surprised himself at Winged Foot. "To be honest with you, this is the last one I would have thought I could win," he said, "because I don't drive very straight, and I demonstrated that on the last nine holes."

Surrounded by spectators, Ogilvy walks to the 18th green after pitching close for what would be the winning putt.

In truth, he drove as well on the first nine as on the second, and indeed those tee shots were not things of beauty. Just three of his drives caught fairways on each nine. Nor did his short game win a prize. Of the last six holes, with the tension at its peak, his approaches found only the 15th green.

Through his career, Ogilvy had been outshone by his countrymen. He ranked 50th in the world standings and sixth among Australians at the start of 2006. Now he stood eighth in the world and second among Australians to Scott, who ranked sixth. Scott had won The Players Championship in 2004, and overall had won three events on the PGA Tour and five on the European Tour.

All his success couldn't mask Scott's dismal record in the Open. Of the five he has played, he missed the cut in his first three, tied for 28th at Pinehurst and for 21st at Winged Foot.

Still, Ogilvy has taken a cautious assessment of his winning. Thinking back on the blunders of Jim Furyk, Montgomerie and especially Mickelson, he admitted he caught a sizable portion of luck.

Assessing his own finish, he felt he'd put himself in trouble at the 17th, when after three shots his ball still hadn't caught the green.

"I thought four over would be the number," Ogilvy said, "because Monty just birdied the 17th, and he and Mickelson would finish at about three or four over." Then, "Yeah. Wow. I chipped in. Just scary. I mean a shot that you wait your whole life to chip in in a situation like that — when you need to — and then you do it." When asked his reaction to winning, Ogilvy claimed, "It's ridiculous. I can't even imagine it."

Baker-Finch had predicted Ogilvy's victory on television the previous week. He thought of how others would look at Ogilvy. "For Geoff's sake," he said, "I hope people don't remember the Open for Monty and Mickelson both making double bogeys."

They should all remember the comment of Cary Middlecoff, the 1949 and 1956 U.S. Open champion: "You don't win the Open," Middlecoff stated. "The Open wins you."

June 15-18, 2006, Winged Foot Golf Club, Mamaroneck, N.Y.

Rd. 1	Rd. 2	Rd. 3	Rd. 4	Contestant		Rounds			Total	Prize
T7	T3	3	1	Geoff Ogilvy	71	70	72	72	285	$1,225,000.00
T2	T5	T8	T2	Jim Furyk	70	72	74	70	286	501,249.00
1	2	T4	T2	Colin Montgomerie	69	71	75	71	286	501,249.00
T2	T7	T1	T2	Phil Mickelson	70	73	69	74	286	501,249.00
T28	T5	T8	5	Padraig Harrington	73	69	74	71	287	255,642.00
T52	T14	T20	T6	Nick O'Hern	75	70	74	69	288	183,255.00
T39	T29	T20	T6	Jeff Sluman	74	73	72	69	288	183,255.00
T7	T14	T8	T6	Mike Weir	71	74	71	72	288	183,255.00
T2	1	T4	T6	Steve Stricker	70	69	76	73	288	183,255.00
T7	T14	T4	T6	Vijay Singh	71	74	70	73	288	183,255.00
T7	T3	T1	T6	Kenneth Ferrie	71	70	71	76	288	183,255.00
T68	T53	T16	T12	Ryuji Imada	76	73	69	71	289	131,670.00
T112	T29	T11	T12	Luke Donald	78	69	70	72	289	131,670.00
T39	T14	T4	T12	Ian Poulter	74	71	70	74	289	131,670.00
T90	T53	T37	15	Paul Casey	77	72	72	69	290	116,735.00
T2	T42	T46	T16	David Howell	70	78	74	69	291	99,417.00
T90	T14	T32	T16	David Duval	77	68	75	71	291	99,417.00
T2	T14	T20	T16	Miguel Angel Jimenez	70	75	74	72	291	99,417.00
T28	T29	T20	T16	Robert Allenby	73	74	72	72	291	99,417.00
T52	T7	T11	T16	Arron Oberholser	75	68	74	74	291	99,417.00
T52	T42	T37	T21	Jose Maria Olazabal	75	73	73	71	292	74,252.00
T127	T53	T37	T21	Tom Pernice Jr.	79	70	72	71	292	74,252.00
T15	T42	T16	T21	Adam Scott	72	76	70	74	292	74,252.00
T15	T21	T11	T21	Peter Hedblom	72	74	71	75	292	74,252.00
T68	T29	T11	T21	Trevor Immelman	76	71	70	75	292	74,252.00
T68	T42	T46	T26	Sean O'Hair	76	72	74	71	293	52,341.00
T39	T29	T37	T26	Ernie Els	74	73	74	72	293	52,341.00
T39	T29	T37	T26	Angel Cabrera	74	73	74	72	293	52,341.00
T112	T53	T32	T26	Ted Purdy	78	71	71	73	293	52,341.00
T52	T21	T20	T26	Henrik Stenson	75	71	73	74	293	52,341.00
T15	T29	T20	T26	Craig Barlow	72	75	72	74	293	52,341.00
T28	T42	T50	T32	Rod Pampling	73	75	75	71	294	41,912.00
T15	T42	T32	T32	Woody Austin	72	76	72	74	294	41,912.00
T15	T11	T20	T32	Scott Hend	72	72	75	75	294	41,912.00
T39	T42	T20	T32	Steve Jones	74	74	71	75	294	41,912.00
T15	T11	T11	T32	Bart Bryant	72	72	73	77	294	41,912.00
T52	T21	T50	T37	Stewart Cink	75	71	77	72	295	36,647.00
T52	T29	T37	T37	Jay Haas	75	72	74	74	295	36,647.00
T90	T42	T37	T37	Charles Howell III	77	71	73	74	295	36,647.00
T68	T53	T59	T40	Stephen Gangluff	76	73	77	70	296	29,459.00
T127	T53	T50	T40	Tommy Armour III	79	70	74	73	296	29,459.00
T7	T53	T50	T40	John Cook	71	78	74	73	296	29,459.00
T15	T3	T37	T40	Jason Dufner	72	71	78	75	296	29,459.00

Rd. 1	Rd. 2	Rd. 3	Rd. 4	Contestant	Rounds				Total	Prize
T52	T42	T37	T40	Lee Williams	75	73	73	75	296	29,459.00
T15	T29	T32	T40	Bo Van Pelt	72	75	73	76	296	29,459.00
T7	T21	T20	T40	Fred Funk	71	75	73	77	296	29,459.00
T68	T29	T20	T40	Chad Collins	76	71	72	77	296	29,459.00
T68	T21	T55	T48	Charley Hoffman	76	70	78	73	297	20,482.00
T39	T21	T46	T48	Charl Schwartzel	74	72	76	75	297	20,482.00
T39	T29	T46	T48	J.B. Holmes	74	73	75	75	297	20,482.00
T28	T29	T32	T48	Kent Jones	73	74	73	77	297	20,482.00
T15	T11	T20	T48	Phillip Archer	72	72	75	78	297	20,482.00
T15	T21	T20	T48	Thomas Bjorn	72	74	73	78	297	20,482.00
T7	T7	T16	T48	Graeme McDowell	71	72	75	79	297	20,482.00
T28	T29	T16	T48	Fred Couples	73	74	71	79	297	20,482.00
T28	T14	T55	56	Darren Clarke	73	72	79	74	298	18,031.00
T112	T53	T59	57	Ben Curtis	78	71	77	73	299	17,614.00
T90	T42	62	58	Kenny Perry	77	71	79	74	301	17,281.00
T28	T53	T59	T59	Jeev Milkha Singh	73	76	77	76	302	16,676.00
T39	T21	58	T59	Camilo Villegas	74	72	79	77	302	16,676.00
T28	T42	T55	T59	Skip Kendall	73	75	76	78	302	16,676.00
T90	T53	T50	62	Ben Crane	77	72	74	80	303	16,126.00
T28	T53	63	63	Tim Herron	73	76	79	77	305	15,836.00

Contestant				Contestant				Contestant			
Jay Delsing	78	72	150	Lucas Glover	75	77	152	*Jonathan Moore	77	78	155
Allen Doyle	76	74	150	Justin Leonard	77	75	152	David Berganio Jr.	77	78	155
Stephen Ames	72	78	150	Jyoti Randhawa	77	75	152	Oliver Wilson	80	76	156
Andrew Svoboda	75	75	150	Brett Quigley	80	73	153	Sergio Garcia	78	78	156
Rory Sabbatini	74	76	150	Mark Brooks	78	75	153	Jason Allred	78	78	156
Paul McGinley	74	76	150	*Edoardo Molinari	77	76	153	Travis Hurst	78	78	156
Zach Johnson	73	77	150	Carl Pettersson	77	76	153	D.J. Trahan	75	81	156
Andrew Morse	74	76	150	Tag Ridings	77	76	153	Shingo Katayama	81	75	156
*Alex Coe	77	73	150	Greg Kraft	76	77	153	*Patrick Nagle	81	75	156
Duffy Waldorf	75	76	151	Dustin White	78	75	153	Brad Fritsch	78	78	156
Corey Pavin	76	75	151	Chris Nallen	79	74	153	Stephen Woodard	79	77	156
Stuart Appleby	72	79	151	Nick Dougherty	78	75	153	Graeme Storm	81	76	157
Mark Hensby	73	78	151	Billy Mayfair	72	81	153	Toru Taniguchi	75	82	157
K.J. Choi	76	75	151	Chad Campbell	76	77	153	Michael Harris	76	81	157
John Mallinger	77	74	151	Rocco Mediate	76	77	153	*Tadd Fujikawa	81	77	158
Shaun Micheel	77	74	151	Rich Beem	74	79	153	Maarten Lafeber	76	83	159
Tim Clark	77	74	151	Ben Hayes	76	77	153	Mark Calcavecchia	80	79	159
Dean Wilson	76	75	151	John Koskinen	79	74	153	George McNeill	77	82	159
Tadahiro Takayama	77	75	152	Matt Kuchar	78	76	154	Mathew Goggin	81	78	159
Bob Estes	80	72	152	Tom Lehman	78	76	154	Nick Price	81	78	159
Tiger Woods	76	76	152	Niclas Fasth	78	76	154	Phil Tataurangi	86	73	159
Michael Campbell	75	77	152	Lee Janzen	82	72	154	David Oh	83	77	160
Olin Browne	80	72	152	J.J. Henry	77	77	154	*Dillon Dougherty	85	75	160
Chris DiMarco	76	76	152	Steve Lowery	79	75	154	*Ryan Baca	78	83	161
Peter Jacobsen	76	76	152	Keiichiro Fukabori	75	79	154	Michael Derminio	81	80	161
Kevin Stadler	71	81	152	Davis Love III	76	78	154	Madalitso Muthiya	81	80	161
Taylor Wood	74	78	152	Joey Sindelar	79	76	155	*Ryan Posey	84	78	162
Nathan Green	77	75	152	Todd Hamilton	77	78	155	Andy Bare	84	78	162
*Billy Horschel	75	77	152	Nicholas Thompson	81	74	155	John Rollins	83	80	163
Brandt Jobe	76	76	152	Richard Green	75	80	155	Rob Johnson	82	82	164
Scott Verplank	76	76	152	Retief Goosen	77	78	155	David Toms	79		WD

Professionals not returning 72-hole scores received $2,000 each.

*Denotes amateur.

106th U.S. OPEN Statistics

Hole	1	2	3	4	5	6	7	8	9	10	11	12	13	14	15	16	17	18	Total	
Par	4	4	3	4	5	4	3	4	4	3	4	5	3	4	4	4	4	4	70	
Geoff Ogilvy																				
Round 1	4	4	[4]	[5]	(4)	[5]	3	4	4	(2)	(3)	5	3	4	4	4	4	[5]	71	
Round 2	4	4	3	[5]	5	4	3	(3)	4	3	[5]	5	3	[5]	(3)	(3)	4	4	70	
Round 3	[5]	4	3	4	5	4	3	4	4	(2)	4	5	[4]	[5]	4	4	4	4	72	
Round 4	4	4	3	4	(4)	(3)	3	[5]	[5]	3	[5]	5	3	[5]	4	4	4	4	72	285
Jim Furyk																				
Round 1	4	4	[4]	[5]	(4)	(3)	3	4	4	(2)	4	5	3	[5]	4	(3)	4	[5]	70	
Round 2	4	[5]	(2)	4	(4)	[5]	3	[5]	4	[4]	4	5	3	4	4	4	4	4	72	
Round 3	4	4	3	4	5	[5]	3	4	4	[5]	4	5	3	4	(3)	[5]	[5]	4	74	
Round 4	(3)	4	3	4	(4)	4	[4]	4	[5]	3	(3)	(4)	3	4	[5]	4	4	[5]	70	286
Colin Montgomerie																				
Round 1	[5]	4	[4]	4	5	(3)	3	[5]	(3)	3	4	(4)	3	4	4	4	(3)	4	69	
Round 2	4	4	3	4	5	4	3	4	4	3	4	5	3	[5]	4	4	4	4	71	
Round 3	[5]	[5]	[5]	[5]	(4)	[5]	3	4	4	3	4	5	3	(3)	4	[5]	4	4	75	
Round 4	4	4	3	(3)	(4)	4	3	4	4	[4]	4	5	3	[5]	4	4	(3)	[6]	71	286
Phil Mickelson																				
Round 1	4	[5]	3	4	5	4	(2)	4	4	3	4	[6]	3	4	4	4	4	(3)	70	
Round 2	[5]	[5]	3	4	5	4	3	4	[5]	3	4	5	(2)	4	4	4	4	[5]	73	
Round 3	4	4	[4]	(3)	5	(3)	3	[5]	[5]	3	4	5	3	(3)	4	(3)	4	4	69	
Round 4	4	4	3	(3)	[6]	4	[4]	4	[5]	3	(3)	5	[4]	(3)	4	[5]	4	[6]	74	286

◯ Circled numbers represent birdies or eagles.　　☐ Squared numbers represent bogeys or worse.

Hole	Yards	Par	Eagles	Birdies	Pars	Bogeys	Double Bogeys	Higher	Average
1	450	4	0	18	234	150	31	4	4.471
2	453	4	0	25	236	154	20	2	4.400
3	216	3	1	16	257	147	16	0	3.368
4	469	4	0	37	234	145	18	3	4.350
5	515	5	10	174	215	35	1	2	4.654
6	321	4	5	59	265	97	11	0	4.114
7	162	3	0	45	316	67	9	0	3.092
8	475	4	0	22	238	166	10	1	4.382
9	514	4	1	26	235	153	20	2	4.391
OUT	3575	35	17	422	2230	1114	136	14	37.222
10	188	3	0	24	261	141	10	1	3.320
11	396	4	1	65	271	76	23	1	4.133
12	640	5	1	49	265	95	20	7	5.243
13	214	3	0	41	271	110	14	1	3.231
14	458	4	0	25	215	174	19	4	4.458
15	416	4	0	43	254	121	18	1	4.268
16	478	4	0	43	218	154	21	1	4.357
17	449	4	1	34	263	117	21	1	4.288
18	450	4	0	20	227	160	24	6	4.471
IN	3689	35	3	344	2245	1148	170	23	37.769
TOTAL	7264	70	20	766	4475	2262	306	37	74.991

106th
U.S. OPEN
Past Results

Date	Winner	Score	Runner-Up	Venue
1895	Horace Rawlins	173 - 36 holes	Willie Dunn	Newport GC, Newport, R.I.
1896	James Foulis	152 - 36 holes	Horace Rawlins	Shinnecock Hills GC, Southampton, N.Y.
1897	Joe Lloyd	162 - 36 holes	Willie Anderson	Chicago GC, Wheaton, Ill.
1898	Fred Herd	328 - 72 holes	Alex Smith	Myopia Hunt Club, S. Hamilton, Mass.
1899	Willie Smith	315	George Low Val Fitzjohn W.H. Way	Baltimore CC, Baltimore, Md.
1900	Harry Vardon	313	J.H. Taylor	Chicago GC, Wheaton, Ill.
1901	*Willie Anderson (85)	331	Alex Smith (86)	Myopia Hunt Club, S. Hamilton, Mass.
1902	Laurie Auchterlonie	307	Stewart Gardner	Garden City GC, Garden City, N.Y.
1903	*Willie Anderson (82)	307	David Brown (84)	Baltusrol GC, Springfield, N.J.
1904	Willie Anderson	303	Gil Nicholls	Glen View Club, Golf, Ill.
1905	Willie Anderson	314	Alex Smith	Myopia Hunt Club, S. Hamilton, Mass.
1906	Alex Smith	295	Willie Smith	Onwentsia Club, Lake Forest, Ill.
1907	Alex Ross	302	Gil Nicholls	Philadelphia Cricket Club, Chestnut Hill, Pa.
1908	*Fred McLeod (77)	322	Willie Smith (83)	Myopia Hunt Club, S. Hamilton, Mass.
1909	George Sargent	290	Tom McNamara	Englewood GC, Englewood, N.J.
1910	*Alex Smith (71)	298	John J. McDermott (75) Macdonald Smith (77)	Philadelphia Cricket Club, Chestnut Hill, Pa.
1911	*John J. McDermott (80)	307	Michael J. Brady (82) George O. Simpson (85)	Chicago GC, Wheaton, Ill.
1912	John J. McDermott	294	Tom McNamara	CC of Buffalo, Buffalo, N.Y.
1913	*Francis Ouimet (72)	304	Harry Vardon (77) Edward Ray (78)	The Country Club, Brookline, Mass.
1914	Walter Hagen	290	Charles Evans Jr.	Midlothian CC, Blue Island, Ill.
1915	Jerome D. Travers	297	Tom McNamara	Baltusrol GC, Springfield, N.J.
1916	Charles Evans Jr.	286	Jock Hutchinson	Minikahda Club, Minneapolis, Minn.
1917-18	No Championships Played — World War I			
1919	*Walter Hagen (77)	301	Michael J. Brady (78)	Brae Burn CC, West Newton, Mass.
1920	Edward Ray	295	Harry Vardon Jack Burke Sr. Leo Diegel Jock Hutchison	Inverness Club, Toledo, Ohio
1921	James M. Barnes	289	Walter Hagen Fred McLeod	Columbia CC, Chevy Chase, Md.
1922	Gene Sarazen	288	John L. Black Robert T. Jones Jr.	Skokie CC, Glencoe, Ill.
1923	*Robert T. Jones Jr. (76)	296	Bobby Cruickshank (78)	Inwood CC, Inwood, N.Y.
1924	Cyril Walker	297	Robert T. Jones Jr.	Oakland Hills CC, Birmingham, Mich.
1925	*William Macfarlane (147)	291	Robert T. Jones Jr. (148)	Worcester CC, Worcester, Mass.
1926	Robert T. Jones Jr.	293	Joe Turnesa	Scioto CC, Columbus, Ohio
1927	*Tommy Armour (76)	301	Harry Cooper (79)	Oakmont CC, Oakmont, Pa.
1928	*Johnny Farrell (143)	294	Robert T. Jones Jr. (144)	Olympia Fields CC, Matteson, Ill.
1929	*Robert T. Jones Jr. (141)	294	Al Espinosa (164)	Winged Foot GC, Mamaroneck, N.Y.

Date	Winner	Score	Runner-Up	Venue
1930	Robert T. Jones Jr.	287	Macdonald Smith	Interlachen CC, Hopkins, Minn.
1931	*Billy Burke (149-148)	292	George Von Elm (149-149)	Inverness Club, Toledo, Ohio
1932	Gene Sarazen	286	Phil Perkins Bobby Cruickshank	Fresh Meadows CC, Flushing, N.Y.
1933	Johnny Goodman	287	Ralph Guldahl	North Shore CC, Glenview, Ill.
1934	Olin Dutra	293	Gene Sarazen	Merion Cricket Club, Ardmore, Pa.
1935	Sam Parks Jr.	299	Jimmy Thomson	Oakmont CC, Oakmont, Pa.
1936	Tony Manero	282	Harry Cooper	Baltusrol GC, Springfield, N.J.
1937	Ralph Guldahl	281	Sam Snead	Oakland Hills CC, Birmingham, Mich.
1938	Ralph Guldahl	284	Dick Metz	Cherry Hills CC, Englewood, Colo.
1939	*Byron Nelson (68-70)	284	Craig Wood (68-73) Denny Shute (76)	Philadelphia CC, West Conshohocken, Pa.
1940	*Lawson Little (70)	287	Gene Sarazen (73)	Canterbury GC, Cleveland, Ohio
1941	Craig Wood	284	Denny Shute	Colonial Club, Fort Worth, Texas
1942-45 No Championships Played — World War II				
1946	*Lloyd Mangrum (72-72)	284	Vic Ghezzi (72-73) Byron Nelson (72-73)	Canterbury GC, Cleveland, Ohio
1947	*Lew Worsham (69)	282	Sam Snead (70)	St. Louis CC, Clayton, Mo.
1948	Ben Hogan	276	Jimmy Demaret	Riviera CC, Los Angeles, Calif.
1949	Cary Middlecoff	286	Sam Snead Clayton Heafner	Medinah CC, Medinah, Ill.
1950	*Ben Hogan (69)	287	Lloyd Mangrum (73) George Fazio (75)	Merion GC, Ardmore, Pa.
1951	Ben Hogan	287	Clayton Heafner	Oakland Hills CC, Birmingham, Mich.
1952	Julius Boros	281	Ed Oliver	Northwood CC, Dallas, Texas
1953	Ben Hogan	283	Sam Snead	Oakmont CC, Oakmont, Pa.
1954	Ed Furgol	284	Gene Littler	Baltusrol GC, Springfield, N.J.
1955	*Jack Fleck (69)	287	Ben Hogan (72)	The Olympic Club, San Francisco, Calif.
1956	Cary Middlecoff	281	Ben Hogan Julius Boros	Oak Hill CC, Rochester, N.Y.
1957	*Dick Mayer (72)	282	Cary Middlecoff (79)	Inverness Club, Toledo, Ohio
1958	Tommy Bolt	283	Gary Player	Southern Hills CC, Tulsa, Okla.
1959	Billy Casper	282	Bob Rosburg	Winged Foot GC, Mamaroneck, N.Y.
1960	Arnold Palmer	280	Jack Nicklaus	Cherry Hills CC, Englewood, Colo.
1961	Gene Littler	281	Bob Goalby Doug Sanders	Oakland Hills CC, Birmingham, Mich.
1962	*Jack Nicklaus (71)	283	Arnold Palmer (74)	Oakmont CC, Oakmont, Pa.
1963	*Julius Boros (70)	293	Jacky Cupit (73) Arnold Palmer (76)	The Country Club, Brookline, Mass.
1964	Ken Venturi	278	Tommy Jacobs	Congressional CC, Bethesda, Md.
1965	*Gary Player (71)	282	Kel Nagle (74)	Bellerive CC, St. Louis, Mo.
1966	*Billy Casper (69)	278	Arnold Palmer (73)	The Olympic Club, San Francisco, Calif.
1967	Jack Nicklaus	275	Arnold Palmer	Baltusrol GC, Springfield, N.J.
1968	Lee Trevino	275	Jack Nicklaus	Oak Hill CC, Rochester, N.Y.
1969	Orville Moody	281	Deane Beman Al Geiberger Bob Rosburg	Champions GC, Houston, Texas
1970	Tony Jacklin	281	Dave Hill	Hazeltine National GC, Chaska, Minn.
1971	*Lee Trevino (68)	280	Jack Nicklaus (71)	Merion GC, Ardmore, Pa.
1972	Jack Nicklaus	290	Bruce Crampton	Pebble Beach GL, Pebble Beach, Calif.
1973	Johnny Miller	279	John Schlee	Oakmont CC, Oakmont, Pa.
1974	Hale Irwin	287	Forrest Fezler	Winged Foot GC, Mamaroneck, N.Y.

Date	Winner	Score	Runner-Up	Venue
1975	*Lou Graham (71)	287	John Mahaffey (73)	Medinah CC, Medinah, Ill.
1976	Jerry Pate	277	Tom Weiskopf Al Geiberger	Atlanta Athletic Club, Duluth, Ga.
1977	Hubert Green	278	Lou Graham	Southern Hills CC, Tulsa, Okla.
1978	Andy North	285	Dave Stockton J.C. Snead	Cherry Hills CC, Englewood, Colo.
1979	Hale Irwin	284	Gary Player Jerry Pate	Inverness Club, Toledo, Ohio
1980	Jack Nicklaus	272	Isao Aoki	Baltusrol GC, Springfield, N.J.
1981	David Graham	273	George Burns Bill Rogers	Merion GC, Ardmore, Pa.
1982	Tom Watson	282	Jack Nicklaus	Pebble Beach GL, Pebble Beach, Calif.
1983	Larry Nelson	280	Tom Watson	Oakmont CC, Oakmont, Pa.
1984	*Fuzzy Zoeller (67)	276	Greg Norman (75)	Winged Foot GC, Mamaroneck, N.Y.
1985	Andy North	279	Dave Barr Chen Tze Chung Denis Watson	Oakland Hills CC, Birmingham, Mich.
1986	Raymond Floyd	279	Lanny Wadkins Chip Beck	Shinnecock Hills GC, Southampton, N.Y.
1987	Scott Simpson	277	Tom Watson	The Olympic Club, San Francisco, Calif.
1988	*Curtis Strange (71)	278	Nick Faldo (75)	The Country Club, Brookline, Mass.
1989	Curtis Strange	278	Chip Beck Mark McCumber Ian Woosnam	Oak Hill CC, Rochester, N.Y.
1990	*Hale Irwin (74+3)	280	Mike Donald (74+4)	Medinah CC, Medinah, Ill.
1991	*Payne Stewart (75)	282	Scott Simpson (77)	Hazeltine National GC, Chaska, Minn.
1992	Tom Kite	285	Jeff Sluman	Pebble Beach GL, Pebble Beach, Calif.
1993	Lee Janzen	272	Payne Stewart	Baltusrol GC, Springfield, N.J.
1994	*Ernie Els (74+4+4)	279	Loren Roberts (74+4+5) Colin Montgomerie (78)	Oakmont CC, Oakmont, Pa.
1995	Corey Pavin	280	Greg Norman	Shinnecock Hills GC, Southampton, N.Y.
1996	Steve Jones	278	Tom Lehman Davis Love III	Oakland Hills CC, Birmingham, Mich.
1997	Ernie Els	276	Colin Montgomerie	Congressional CC, Bethesda, Md.
1998	Lee Janzen	280	Payne Stewart	The Olympic Club, San Francisco, Calif.
1999	Payne Stewart	279	Phil Mickelson	Pinehurst Resort & CC, Pinehurst No. 2, Pinehurst, N.C.
2000	Tiger Woods	272	Miguel Angel Jimenez Ernie Els	Pebble Beach GL, Pebble Beach, Calif.
2001	*Retief Goosen (70)	276	Mark Brooks (72)	Southern Hills CC, Tulsa, Okla.
2002	Tiger Woods	277	Phil Mickelson	Bethpage State Park, Farmingdale, N.Y.
2003	Jim Furyk	272	Stephen Leaney	Olympia Fields CC, Olympia Fields, Ill.
2004	Retief Goosen	276	Phil Mickelson	Shinnecock Hills GC, Southampton, N.Y.
2005	Michael Campbell	280	Tiger Woods	Pinehurst Resort & CC, Pinehurst No. 2, Pinehurst, N.C.
2006	Geoff Ogilvy	285	Jim Furyk Phil Mickelson Colin Montgomerie	Winged Foot GC, Mamaroneck, N.Y.

*Winner in playoff; figures in parentheses indicate scores

106th
U.S. OPEN
Championship Records

Oldest champion *(years/months/days)*
  45/0/15 — Hale Irwin (1990)
Youngest champion
  19/10/14 — John J. McDermott (1911)
Most victories
  4 — Willie Anderson (1901, '03, '04, '05)
  4 — Robert T. Jones Jr. (1923, '26, '29, '30)
  4 — Ben Hogan (1948, '50, '51, '53)
  4 — Jack Nicklaus (1962, '67, '72, '80)
  3 — Hale Irwin (1974, '79, '90)
  2 — by 16 players: Alex Smith (1906, '10), John J.
    McDermott (1911, '12), Walter Hagen (1914,
    '19), Gene Sarazen (1922, '32), Ralph Guldahl
    (1937, '38), Cary Middlecoff (1949, '56), Julius
    Boros (1952, '63), Billy Casper (1959, '66), Lee
    Trevino (1968, '71), Andy North (1978, '85),
    Curtis Strange (1988, '89), Ernie Els (1994,
    '97), Lee Janzen (1993, '98), Payne Stewart
    (1991, '99), Tiger Woods (2000, '02) and
    Retief Goosen (2001, '04)
Consecutive victories
  3 — Willie Anderson (1903, '04, '05)
  2 — John J. McDermott (1911, '12)
  2 — Robert T. Jones Jr. (1929, '30)
  2 — Ralph Guldahl (1937, '38)
  2 — Ben Hogan (1950, '51)
  2 — Curtis Strange (1988, '89)
Most times runner-up
  4 — Sam Snead
  4 — Robert T. Jones Jr.
  4 — Arnold Palmer
  4 — Jack Nicklaus
  4 — Phil Mickelson
Longest course
  7,264 yards — Winged Foot Golf Club (West
    Course), Mamaroneck, N.Y. (2006)
Shortest course
  Since World War II
  6,528 yards — Merion GC (East Course),
    Ardmore, Pa. (1971, '81)
Most often host club of Open
  7 — Baltusrol GC, Springfield, N.J. (1903, '15, '36,
    '54, '67, '80, '93)
  7 — Oakmont (Pa.) CC (1927, '35, '53, '62, '73, '83,
    '94)
Largest entry
  9,048 (2005)
Smallest entry
  11 (1895)
Lowest score, 72 holes
  272 — Jack Nicklaus (63-71-70-68), at Baltusrol
    GC (Lower Course), Springfield, N.J. (1980)

  272 — Lee Janzen (67-67-69-69), at Baltusrol GC
    (Lower Course), Springfield, N.J. (1993)
  272 — Tiger Woods (65-69-71-67), at Pebble
    Beach (Calif.) GL (2000)
  272 — Jim Furyk (67-66-67-72), at Olympia Fields
    (Ill.) CC (North Course) (2003)
Lowest score, first 54 holes
  200 — Jim Furyk (67-66-67), at Olympia Fields
    (Ill.) CC (North Course) (2003)
Lowest score, last 54 holes
  203 — Loren Roberts (69-64-70), at Oakmont
    (Pa.) CC (1994)
Lowest score, first 36 holes
  133 — Vijay Singh (70-63), at Olympia Fields (Ill.)
    CC (North Course) (2003)
  133 — Jim Furyk (67-66), at Olympia Fields (Ill.)
    CC (North Course) (2003)
Lowest score, last 36 holes
  132 — Larry Nelson (65-67), at Oakmont (Pa.) CC
    (1983)
Lowest score, 9 holes
  29 — Neal Lancaster (second nine, fourth round)
    at Shinnecock Hills GC, Southampton, N.Y.
    (1995)
  29 — Neal Lancaster (second nine, second round)
    at Oakland Hills CC, Birmingham, Mich.
    (1996)
  29 — Vijay Singh (second nine, second round),
    at Olympia Fields (Ill.) CC (North Course)
    (2003)
Lowest score, 18 holes
  63 — Johnny Miller, fourth round at Oakmont
    (Pa.) CC (1973)
  63 — Jack Nicklaus, first round at Baltusrol GC
    (Lower Course), Springfield, N.J. (1980)
  63 — Tom Weiskopf, first round at Baltusrol GC
    (Lower Course), Springfield, N.J. (1980)
  63 — Vijay Singh, second round at Olympia Fields
    (Ill.) CC (North Course) (2003)
Largest winning margin
  15 — Tiger Woods (272), at Pebble Beach (Calif.)
    GL (2000)
Highest winning score
  Since World War II
  293 — Julius Boros, at The Country Club,
    Brookline, Mass. (1963) (won in playoff)
Best start by champion
  63 — Jack Nicklaus, at Baltusrol GC (Lower
    Course), Springfield, N.J. (1980)
Best finish by champion
  63 — Johnny Miller, at Oakmont (Pa.) CC (1973)

Worst start by champion
Since World War II
76 — Ben Hogan, at Oakland Hills CC (South Course), Birmingham, Mich. (1951)
76 — Jack Fleck, at The Olympic Club (Lake Course), San Francisco, Calif. (1955)

Worst finish by champion
Since World War II
75 — Cary Middlecoff, at Medinah (Ill.) CC (No. 3 Course) (1949)
75 — Hale Irwin, at Inverness Club, Toledo, Ohio (1979)

Lowest score to lead field, 18 holes
63 — Jack Nicklaus and Tom Weiskopf, at Baltusrol GC (Lower Course), Springfield, N.J. (1980)

Lowest score to lead field, 36 holes
133 — Vijay Singh (70-63) and Jim Furyk (67-66), at Olympia Fields (Ill.) CC (North Course) (2003)

Lowest score to lead field, 54 holes
200 — Jim Furyk (67-66-67), at Olympia Fields (Ill.) CC (North Course) (2003)

Highest score to lead field, 18 holes
Since World War II
71 — Sam Snead, at Oakland Hills CC (South Course), Birmingham, Mich. (1951)
71 — Tommy Bolt, Julius Boros, and Dick Metz, at Southern Hills CC, Tulsa, Okla. (1958)
71 — Tony Jacklin, at Hazeltine National GC, Chaska, Minn. (1970)
71 — Orville Moody, Jack Nicklaus, Chi Chi Rodriguez, Mason Rudolph, Tom Shaw, and Kermit Zarley, at Pebble Beach (Calif.) GL (1972)

Highest score to lead field, 36 holes
Since World War II
144 — Bobby Locke (73-71), at Oakland Hills CC (South Course), Birmingham, Mich. (1951)
144 — Tommy Bolt (67-77) and E. Harvie Ward (74-70), at The Olympic Club (Lake Course), San Francisco, Calif. (1955)
144 — Homero Blancas (74-70), Bruce Crampton (74-70), Jack Nicklaus (71-73), Cesar Seduno (72-72), Lanny Wadkins (76-68) and Kermit Zarley (71-73), at Pebble Beach (Calif.) GL (1972)

Highest score to lead field, 54 holes
Since World War II
218 — Bobby Locke (73-71-74), at Oakland Hills CC (South Course), Birmingham, Mich. (1951)
218 — Jacky Cupit (70-72-76), at The Country Club, Brookline, Mass. (1963)

Lowest 36-hole cut
143 — at Olympia Fields (Ill.) CC (North Course) (2003)

Highest 36-hole cut
155 — at The Olympic Club (Lakeside Course), San Francisco, Calif. (1955)

Most players to tie for lead, 18 holes
7 — at Pebble Beach (Calif.) GL (1972); at Southern Hills CC, Tulsa, Okla. (1977); and at Shinnecock Hills GC, Southampton, N.Y. (1896)

Most players to tie for lead, 36 holes
6 — at Pebble Beach (Calif.) GL (1972)

Most players to tie for lead, 54 holes
4 — at Oakmont (Pa.) CC (1973)

Most sub-par rounds, championship
124 — at Medinah (Ill.) CC (No. 3 Course) (1990)

Most sub-par 72-hole totals, championship
28 — at Medinah (Ill.) CC (No. 3 Course) (1990)

Most sub-par scores, first round
39 — at Medinah (Ill.) CC (No. 3 Course) (1990)

Most sub-par scores, second round
47 — at Medinah (Ill.) CC (No. 3 Course) (1990)

Most sub-par scores, third round
24 — at Medinah (Ill.) CC (No. 3 Course) (1990)

Most sub-par scores, fourth round
18 — at Baltusrol GC (Lower Course), Springfield, N.J. (1993)

Most sub-par rounds by one player in one championship
4 — Billy Casper, at The Olympic Club (Lakeside Course), San Francisco, Calif. (1966)
4 — Lee Trevino, at Oak Hill CC (East Course), Rochester, N.Y. (1968)
4 — Tony Jacklin, at Hazeltine National GC, Chaska, Minn. (1970)
4 — Lee Janzen, at Baltusrol GC (Lower Course), Springfield, N.J. (1993)

Highest score, one hole
19 — Ray Ainsley, at the 16th (par 4) at Cherry Hills CC, Englewood, Colo. (1938)

Most consecutive birdies
6 — George Burns (holes 2–7), at Pebble Beach (Calif.) GL (1972) and Andy Dillard (holes 1–6), at Pebble Beach (Calif.) GL (1992)

Most consecutive 3s
7 — Hubert Green (holes 10–16), at Southern Hills Country Club, Tulsa, Okla. (1977)
7 — Peter Jacobsen (holes 1–7), at The Country Club, Brookline, Mass. (1988)

Most consecutive Opens
44 — Jack Nicklaus (1957-2000)

Most Opens completed 72 holes
35 — Jack Nicklaus

Most consecutive Opens completed 72 holes
22 — Walter Hagen (1913-36; no championships 1917-18)
22 — Gene Sarazen (1920-41)
22 — Gary Player (1958-79)

Robert Sommers is the former editor and publisher of the USGA's *Golf Journal*, author of *The U.S. Open: Golf's Ultimate Challenge* and *Golf Anecdotes*. He is based in Port St. Lucie, Fla.

The photographers and technicians of **Getty Images** who contributed to this publication are **Rebecca Butala, Scott Halleran, Richard Heathcote, Nick Laham, Travis Lindquist, Ezra Shaw** and **Jamie Squire**.

106th U.S. Open Championship

Winged Foot Golf Club

June 15-18, 2006

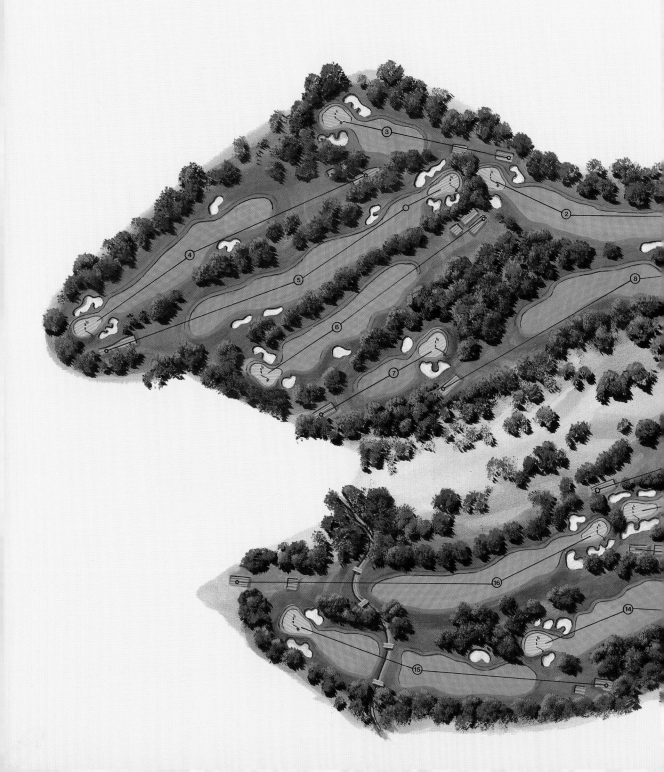